FELLOWSHIP FOUNDATIONS

Basic Doctrine and Polity of the
International Fellowship of Bible Churches, Inc.

Prepared as a Teaching Guide for Basic Christian Doctrine,
and also as a guide for Preparation for Ordination within the
International Fellowship of Bible Churches, Inc.

By

Dr. William Sillings
with
Dr. Vic Reasoner

IFBC Publishers
PO Box 1222
Bethany, OK 73008

© 2003 International Fellowship of Bible Churches, Inc.
ISBN 0-9740229-0-X

Library of Congress Control Number: 2003105180

TABLE OF CONTENTS

Foreword *by Dr. Donald E. Hicks*. 5
Introduction. 7
    The Need in the Pew 7
    The Need in the Pulpit. 8
Part 1. Basic Theological Beliefs. 9
    Introduction 9
    Chapter One   Revelation 10
                            1. General Revelation 10
                            2. Special Revelation 11
                            3. Inspiration 13
                            4. Inerrancy 14
                            5. The Authority of Scripture 14
                            6. The Sufficiency of Scripture 15
    Chapter Two   The Doctrine of God 17
                            1. The Revelation of God's Nature . . 17
                            2. The Work of God 21
    Chapter Three The Doctrine of Christ 23
                            1. The Person of Christ 23
                            2. The Humanity of Christ 25
                            3. The Deity of Christ 25
                            4. The Work of Christ 26
    Chapter Four   The Doctrine of the Holy Spirit 30
                            1. His Personality. 30
                            2. His Deity 30
                            3. His Ministry 31
    Chapter Five   The Doctrine of the Trinity. 33
    Chapter Six   The Doctrine of Mankind. 35
                            1. The Creation of Man. 35
                            2. The Image of God 35
    Chapter Seven The Doctrine of Sin 37
                            1. Sin Defined. 37
                            2. The Fall of Man 39
                            3. Total Depravity 40
    Chapter Eight The Doctrine of the Atonement 43
                            1. The Necessity of the Atonement . . 43
                            2. The Atonement as Substitution. . . 44
                            3. The Atonement as Satisfaction . . . 45
                            4. The Extent of the Atonement 45

Chapter Nine	The Doctrine of Salvation	46
	1. The Divine Initiative	46
	2. The Human Response	49
	3. The New Birth	51
	4. Christian Security	54
Chapter Ten	The Doctrine of Sanctification	56
	1. Stages of Christian Sanctification	58
	2. The Experience of Entire Sanctification and the Life of Holiness	60
	3. Crisis and Process	63
	4. Entire Sanctification/Perfecting Grace	64
	5. Ethical and Moral Purity	65
	6. The Gift of Tongues	65
	7. What God's Sanctifying Grace Can Do For You	67
Chapter Eleven	The Doctrine of the Church	69
	1. The Origin of the Church	69
	2. The Marks of the Church	69
	3. The Essential Characteristics of the Church	70
	4. The Ministry of the Church; Gifts of the Spirit	74
	5. The Sacraments	75
	6. The Mission of the Church	76
Chapter Twelve	The Doctrine of Last Things	79
	1. Five Prophetic Fundamentals	79

Part 2. Fellowship History 83
　The Apostles Creed 83
　The Nicene Creed 84
　The Athanasian Creed 84
　Organizational Beginnings 88
　Missions 90
Part 3. Fellowship Polity 91
　Offices of the Church 93
　The Call of God and the Recognition of the Church . . . 96
Part 4. The Ordination Process 97
Part 5. General Operations 103
Part 6. Ministerial Discipline 107
Conclusion 111

FOREWORD

This volume, *Fellowship Foundations*, provides an overview of foundational truths and guiding principles on which the International Fellowship of Bible Churches is established. It defines the theology, polity, vision, and objectives of the International Fellowship of Bible Churches, Inc. For the minister, this volume also provides the necessary theological framework for ordination into a ministry of purpose within the Fellowship.

The principles contained in this volume must be consolidated into our character and mission. It is especially imperative that these core values and disciplines are comprehended, affirmed, mastered, and taught by the ministerial leadership of the International Fellowship of Bible Churches.

The Fellowship recognizes the authority placed upon those called by God to preach the Gospel, particularly in our fragmented twenty-first century culture. The effectiveness with which Fellowship ministers carry out their sacred call will be the distinguishing hallmark of the International Fellowship of Bible Churches.

This divine appointment cannot be viewed lightly, nor shunned recklessly. God's words to Jeremiah define His call with clarity: "Before I formed you in the womb I knew you, before you were born I set you apart; I appointed you as a prophet (minister) to the nations."

Spiritual leadership demands the utmost of one's spiritual qualities and integrity of character, coupled with ongoing development of personal talents and intellect. The benchmark of unity to which both clergy and lay-persons align themselves will determine the effectiveness by which the church's mission and purpose are achieved. It is with the intent of providing such a benchmark for Fellowship theology and practice that this book has been published.

Drs. William Sillings and Vic Reasoner have my deepest appreciation for their preparation of this book to further the ministry of the International Fellowship of Bible Churches, Inc.

Dr. Donald E. Hicks
Fellowship Pastoral Consultant

INTRODUCTION

This book and its corresponding study course are meant to address a common need among two groups of people. First, it is designed to furnish people in the pew a study of basic theological truth in an easily understandable form. Second, it is designed to ensure theological continuity among ministers who wish to be ordained within the International Fellowship of Bible Churches, Inc.

The Need in the Pew

Contemporary American culture tends to be both theologically poor and biblically illiterate, or just slightly literate. People often choose their church affiliations for many reasons other than, or even in spite of, their understanding of the Bible and theology. Some even believe theology really isn't important to the Christian experience. After all, if I can go to a church which has a variant theology and still worship God, isn't that all that really matters?

Not really. In fact, not at all. While one's experience of God begins as a sovereign act of the Almighty God toward us, the truth is that our continuing experience of God, and the lifestyle we choose to follow, depends heavily upon our theology. That is, good biblical theology leads to good worship, while poor theology leads to poor worship. The same principle applies to Christian living: good theology leads to mature Christian living, while poor theology leads to immaturity and spiritual weakness and failure.

For instance, you may attend a church where you have an emotionally rich and exciting experience of worship at the beginning, but in a few weeks or months find it to be quite unsatisfying spiritually. Likewise, you may attend a church where the form of worship is present, and the orthodoxy of the church cannot be questioned, but the worship service is lifeless and does not transform the life.

What is needed is a combination of both vibrant worship and deep theological understanding. In fact, as stated above, long term vibrant worship depends heavily on good theological underpinnings. Why? Worship is a two-way street. It requires time for God to speak to the heart of the worshiper, as well as for the worshiper to sing praise to the heart of God. That requires good biblical understanding of God and sound theological underpinnings. Without these, only an empty emotional shell of worship remains, and the spirit is left dry and helpless.

Thus, one may attend a congregation where the worship style does not reach a high emotional pitch every Sunday, but it is built on deep Scriptural and theologically sound understanding of the Word of God. At first glance, the services may seem less exciting and less emotionally charged than at some other churches. However, within in a few months, the depth of understanding gained through biblical preaching and sound theological underpinnings, deepens your worship of God. Ultimately, this will lead to much greater joy over a long period of time. Your life and spirit will be ultimately transformed through the renewing of your mind by the Word of God.

The Need in the Pulpit

Biblical illiteracy and theological poverty are not problems for people in the pew only, but they are also problematic for those who fill the pulpit. In fact, a good case can be made for the belief that the problem originates in the pulpit and makes its way to the pew. For, over time, the people in the pew reflect what is taught from the pulpit.

For this and other reasons, this book is presented as a standard of theological continuity for Fellowship ministers. While we do not expect conformity in all theological or practical issues, some truths are so basic to Christian understanding that we must all agree if we are to walk together. This book presents the unifying theological truths around which we believe all Fellowship ministers must gather to provide doctrinal and spiritual continuity for our people.

Therefore, this book and its corresponding study course are designed to:
1. Provide a comprehendible compendium of the basic theology, polity, history and praxis of the International Fellowship of Bible Churches, Inc.
2. Equip ministers, church members and teachers with the knowledge to understand, represent and explain the theology and practice of the International Fellowship of Bible Churches, Inc. adequately.
3. Ensure doctrinal and practical compatibility of ordination candidates with the theology and purposes of the International Fellowship of Bible Churches, Inc.

The book and course of study take the following order:
    Part 1.   Basic Theological Beliefs
    Part 2.   Fellowship History
    Part 3.   Fellowship Polity
    Part 4.   The Ordination Process
    Part 5.   General Organizational Operations
    Part 6.   Ministerial Discipline

Basic Theological Beliefs of the International Fellowship of Bible Churches, Inc.

Introduction

Theology is the study of God based upon his self-disclosure. Its focus is God's nature, character, activity, and his relationship to creation — especially man. The purpose of theology is to produce an adequate and consistent expression of the Christian faith. The starting point of Christian theology is God's revelation or disclosure of himself through Scripture. When we observe, collect, and interpret the biblical evidence, we are then able to formulate doctrine and to systematize these doctrines into an understandable and liveable form.

Why is doctrine important?

1.   Some doctrine is essential for salvation. "How can they believe in the one of whom they have not heard?" (Rom 10:9-17).

2.   Correct doctrine is protection against false teaching. Paul indicates that one of the goals of Christian ministry is to mature the saints so that we will not be "blown here and there by every wind of teaching and by the cunning and craftiness of men in their deceitful scheming" (Eph 4:14).

3.   Correct doctrine equips us for service. "All Scripture is God-breathed and useful ... so that the man of God may be thoroughly equipped for every good work" (2 Tim 3:17).

4.   We are commanded to teach all nations (Matt 28:20).

Chapter One

Revelation

God is the first cause of all things. As will be shown in the section on the doctrine of God, he is eternal and exists in eternity before and after all creation. He is uncaused and uncreated. He is the beginning and the beginner of all creation.

Nevertheless, revelation is the actual starting point of theology as we can know it. All truth is God's truth. And revelation begins with God. Thus, if God had not seen fit to reveal Himself to humans, we would know nothing of him or his purposes.

God has revealed himself in several ways:

1. He first revealed himself in personal relationships to human beings, namely to Adam and Eve.
2. He also revealed himself through creation, or natural revelation.
3. Then he revealed himself through the words of the Prophets and Apostles.
4. Finally, according to Hebrews 1:2, he has revealed himself to us through his Son.

The doctrine of revelation is often divided into two large categories — general revelation and special revelation.

1. General Revelation

General revelation is God revealing himself through the means of knowledge which is available to all mankind in general. For instance, there is a general consciousness of God among all men. "He has also set eternity in the hearts of men: yet they cannot fathom what God has done from beginning to end" (Eccl 3:11). Every man who comes into the world somehow encounters some degree of light (John 1:9).

The psalmist spoke of general revelation in delightfully poetic language.

> The heavens declare the glory of God; the skies proclaim the work of his hands. Day after day they pour forth speech; night after night they display knowledge. There is no speech or language where their voice is not heard. Their voice goes out into all the earth, their words to the ends of the world (Psalm 19:1-4).

If we had nothing more than *general revelation*, we could still easily conclude that there must be an intelligent being who had great power. Some philosophers reasoned that there must be one supreme being; others tried to explain the existence of evil by teaching there were two gods. Without the revelation of Genesis 3, we could not explain how evil came into a perfect world created by a good God. "Take away the first three chapters of Genesis and you cannot maintain a true Christian position nor give Christianity's answers" [Francis Schaeffer, *The Complete Works of Francis A. Schaeffer*. Crossway Books, 1982, 1:114].

2. Special Revelation

In contrast to general revelation, the Bible is *special revelation*. Through the Bible, God spent considerable energy and time to reveal his character, his will and purposes, his desire for all, and his plan of salvation through Jesus Christ. While through general revelation we can deduce that there must be a God who is very great and powerful, reading the Scriptures leaves no doubt as to the kind of God he is, nor what he has done and/or what he intends to do with the world and the people he has created. He clearly reveals himself through special revelation.

God's revelation is personal. God did not communicate abstract truth, he revealed himself through people and history. The God of the Bible is not the God of the philosophers, but the God of Abraham, Isaac, and Jacob. He also communicates to us personally through the words of the Scripture.

God's revelation is propositional. Propositional truth is truth communicated in the form of statements which can be affirmed or denied and thus are open to verification. It is good news that God has spoken to us through the Scriptures, and that he condescended to use words we can understand. He did not use technical language. In the Scriptures, God revealed Himself through the most accurate method of communication — writing. He accompanied His revelation with external authentication. The Bible is historically reliable, corresponds to human experience, is true to nature, confirmed by miracles, "God also testified to it by signs, wonders and various miracles, and gifts of the Holy Spirit distributed according to His will" (Heb 2:4), authenticated by fulfilled prophecy — 20-25% of Scriptures was prophetic when given, and affirmed by Jesus Christ, who fulfilled 332 distinct Old Testament prophecies.

God's revelation is also incarnational. The highest point of God's revelation is the incarnate Word of God, Jesus Christ. Through Christ, God has spoken, once-for-all. Having spoken to the prophets through dreams, visions, voices, and angels, "in these last days he has spoken (aorist active indicative) to us by his Son" (Heb 1:2). Yet, even this revelation of the incarnate word is further revealed through the written word in the Bible. Christ, the Word, is the theme of the entire Bible. "Beginning with Moses and all the Prophets, he explained to them what was said in all the Scriptures concerning himself" (Lk 24:27). Furthermore, the church is built upon the "foundation of the apostles and prophets (Old and New Testaments), Jesus Christ himself being the chief cornerstone" (Eph 2:20).

With regard to the doctrine of biblical revelation, it is important to understand four very specific words: inspiration, inerrancy, authority and sufficiency.

1. *Inspiration* means God superintended the human authors, using their individual personalities, so that they composed and recorded without error His revelation to man.

2. *Inerrancy* means that the Bible, as originally given, was free from error and that the human authors accurately recorded what God said.

3. *Authority* means that the Bible is our final authority in all matters of faith and practice because it was inspired by God. The red letters are not more authoritative than the black ones. The Fellowship *Handbook of Faith and Practice* states, "We adopt the Bible, carefully and prayerfully interpreted and applied under the leadership of the Holy Spirit, and in light of the faith and practice of the Church of Christ universal — ancient and contemporary — to be our rule of faith and practice" (See *Handbook*, "Guide to Practice").

4. *Sufficiency* means that the Scripture is sufficient to guide the believer in all matters of faith and practice. No other book is essential to our understanding of Scripture, and whatever is not contained in the Scripture is not to be considered essential to salvation.

3. Inspiration

The written Word of God came over a span of fifteen hundred years through forty human authors representing twenty occupations on three continents in ten countries and in three languages. These men spoke as they were "carried along by the Holy Spirit" (2 Peter 1:21), so that their words came from God and had the ring and authority of the words of God, as though God had spoken the words directly. Isaiah claimed his message came directly from God forty times, Jeremiah claimed the same thing a hundred times and Ezekiel sixty times. The phrase "thus saith the Lord" occurs in the Bible over two thousand times. What a testimony to God's revelation to mankind, through mankind and for mankind!

These holy men acted as secretaries for God. Sometimes they took dictation. Sometimes they did research (see Luke 1:1-4). Sometimes they wrote down their own personal experiences with God. At other times they received supernaturally communicated information, and someone else wrote down their words. As well, God allowed them the use of their own personalities, and their own language and culture were not bypassed. As you read from the original languages of the Scripture, you can see differences in their writing styles. Yet the final product is inspired by God. "All Scripture is God-breathed" (1 Tim 3:16 NIV; "Inspired of God" KJV).

Other books may claim inspiration, but their claims must be evaluated on two bases:

1. External credibility. Do they contain factual errors, hearsay evidence, historical inconsistencies? The books of the Bible were accepted as from God when they were written by a culture who could have spotted factual error easily. Furthermore, God confirmed His word to those who heard it through miracles. "God also testified to it by signs, wonders, and various miracles, and gifts of the Holy Spirit" (Heb 2:4). These were witnessed and experienced by the biblical authors themselves, and witnessed to by many others. No other book of any religion can lay authentic claim to the external credibility held by the Holy Scriptures.

2. Internal consistency. In spite of being written over such a diversity of circumstances, there are no contradictions within the Bible. Furthermore, the substance of the Bible is not trivial, confused, or irrelevant. The message of the Bible points to God and lifts the reader's thoughts to the most important issues. Scripture is not some nonsensical gobbledygook that can only be interpreted mystically by those who are mentally unstable. It carries a majesty fitting of a divine author.

4. Inerrancy

The doctrine of inerrancy claims that God so superintended the process of the production of the Scriptures that the final message of the authors was accurate and without human error. While there exists a wide variety of views of inerrancy, we believe that the Scriptures, as received and produced by the authors of Scripture, were completely accurate in everything pertinent to the communication of God's revelation of truth in written form. Thus, what is revealed in those pages is fully trustworthy.

Psalm 19:7 declares the law of the Lord is perfect. Jesus said the smallest letter or part of a letter would not have to be altered (Matt 5:18). Jesus said that the Word of God is true (John 17:17). John Wesley concluded, "If there be any mistakes in the Bible there may as well be a thousand. If there be one falsehood in that book, it did not come from the God of truth" [*Journal*, 24 July, 1776].

5. The Authority of Scripture

If the Bible is actually revelation from God, and if he so superintended the production of the Scriptures that the original autographs were without error (as we believe and teach), it follows logically and Scripturally that the Bible is the fully trustworthy Word of God. As the revealed and inspired and trustworthy Word of God, the Scripture is fully authoritative in all matters it addresses, especially in all matters relating to faith, salvation and Christian life.

We cannot have more than one ultimate authority. The Bible is our final and sole authority for faith and practice. Tradition, experience, and reason are helpful to theology, but they cannot be the basis or starting point for an adequate theology. They do not carry the weight of Scriptural authority, but they may have value in clarifying our interpretation of Scripture and illustrating the axioms of Scripture.

But couldn't anyone write a book and in it claim that it was from God? Yes, false prophets can write books, but when you read the Bible you will conclude that:

1. Bad men would not have written such a book on their own because they would be condemning themselves.

2. Good men could not have written such a book on their own because good men would not deliberately attempt to deceive.

3. Therefore it must have been inspired by God.

6. The Sufficiency of Scripture

The Holy Spirit was not only active in the revealing and inspiration of Scripture, but he also illuminates the Scriptures to the mind of the believer, making it possible for the believer to receive, understand and apply divine revelation through its pages.

1 Corinthians 2:10-14 states the following: "God has revealed it to us by his Spirit. The Spirit searches all things, even the deep things of God. For who among men knows the thoughts of a man except the man's spirit within him? In the same way no one knows the thoughts of God except the Spirit of God. We have not received the spirit of the world but the Spirit who is from God, that we may understand what God has freely given us. This is what we speak, not in words taught us by human wisdom but in words taught by the Spirit, expressing spiritual truths in spiritual words. The man without the Spirit does not accept the things that come from the Spirit of God, for they are foolishness to him, and he cannot understand them, because they are spiritually discerned" (NIV).

When the Scriptures are accurately understood, interpreted and applied, with the illumination of the Holy Spirit, as well as careful study and discernment, they are completely sufficient for the believer's direction in Christian living. The Bible is of such complete sufficiency that whatever is not contained in its pages is not to be considered essential to the faith or practice of any believer.

✓Interview Question: What is your view of the authority of Scripture?

For Further Reading: *This is the first section for which we make recommendations for further reading. Such recommendations will appear throughout this book. However, we wish to make the following disclaimer. Whereas ministers need to be aware of Christian writers and their works, our recommendations for these sections do not necessarily constitute blanket endorsements of all their writings.*

Lindsell, Harold. *The Battle for the Bible.* Grand Rapids: Zondervan, 1976.

Little, Paul. *Know Why You Believe.* Wheaton, IL: Victor Books, 1967.

Purkiser, W. T., ed. *Exploring Our Christian Faith.* Rev. ed. Kansas City: Beacon Hill, 1978. Chapter 3.

Wakefield, Samuel. *Christian Theology.* 2 vols. 1862. Rpt. Salem, OH: Schmul Publishers, 1985. Book One.

Chapter Two

The Doctrine of God

No people ever rise above their religion and no religion is greater than its concept of God. The essence of idolatry is the entertainment of thoughts about God that are unworthy of Him. "Without doubt, the mightiest thought the mind can entertain is the thought of God, and the weightiest word in any language is its word for God." Our tendency is always to reduce or lower God and exalt man in God's place.

A proper understanding of God is the most important doctrine of the Church. An improper view of God is one reason much of our worship has become shallow; it has become entertainment rather than true worship. Many years ago, A. W. Tozer warned that a loss of the majesty of God would lead to "a hundred lesser evils." He claimed that there was scarcely an error in doctrine or ethics that could not be traced to a wrong concept of God [*The Knowledge of the Holy*, Harper and Row, 1961, pp. 6, 9-10].

1. The Revelation of God's Nature

An *attribute* is something true about God; a description of what God is and how he acts. Each attribute is something God has revealed to us about himself. Please note that God is not the sum total of the attributes we discuss. He has numberless attributes. He is incomprehensible, yet we can pull together several of his characteristics as he revealed them in Scripture.

    A.   Absolute Attributes — qualities he shares with no one

        1A1.   Attributes Concerning his Being

Self-existence - God is living and active. God had no origin; He is dependant upon no one. He alone can declare, "I am because I am" (Exod 3:14). God is self-sufficient and uncreated.

Infinity - We are finite creatures. God has no bounds. "The heavens, even the highest heaven, cannot contain you" (1 Kings 8:27). With regard to space, God is immense or unmeasurable; with regard to time God is eternal.

Spirituality - God is spirit (John 4:24). He does not have a body; he is invisible.

Unity - "The Lord our God, the Lord is one" (Deut 6:4). "There is no God but one" (1 Cor 8:4). This excludes all polytheistic concepts of God.

Eternity - "From everlasting to everlasting you are God" (Psalm 90:2). We are temporal. God is without beginning or ending.

Immutability - He is unchanging. "I the Lord do not change" (Mal 3:6). "Jesus Christ is the same yesterday and today and forever" (Heb 13:8).

1A2. Attributes Concerning His Majesty

Sovereignty - There can be only one absolute ruler. "The Lord will reign for ever and ever" (Exod 15:18). God's sovereignty is not absolute in the sense that he determines all that happens, but relative in the sense that no matter what happens, he knows about it, and will ultimately use it for good to accomplish his eternal purposes. This is not a sign of weakness on God's part, but an indication of his binding himself to the will of human kind. He has made us in his likeness and image, and though this image is darkened by the fall, it includes the ability of mankind to make choices and to affect the short-term actions of God in relationship to his will. Thus, rather than being an indication of weakness on God's part, relative sovereignty is actually an indication of eternal power and majesty.

Omnipresence - "Where can I go from your Spirit? Where can I flee from your presence?" (Psalm 139:7-12). "Do not I fill heaven and earth?" (Jer 23:23-24).

Sometimes God's transcendence and His immanence are made separate categories from omnipresence. He is everywhere present, yet not confined to any one location. Medieval Scholastics said, "God's center is everywhere, God's circumference nowhere."

Omniscience - "His understanding has no limit" (Psalm 147:5).

> O Lord, you have searched me and you know me. You know when I sit and when I rise; you perceive my thoughts from afar. You discern my going out and my lying down; you are familiar with all my ways. Before a word is on my tongue you know it completely, O Lord (Psalm 139:1-4).

Does God know what will happen before it occurs? God has *foreknowledge*. Isaiah 41:21-26 challenges idolaters by asking if their idols could tell what is going to happen. "Tell us what the future holds, so we may know that you are gods." In this contrast it is implied that God alone can tell the future. How else could prophecy be given? (see John 13:19).

1 John 3:20, "God knows everything." God "calls things that are not as though they were" (Rom 4:17). There are examples where the prophets foretold the outcome of more than one choice (see Jer 38:17-18).

Through his foreknowledge, God knew that we would sin and need a Savior (1 Peter 1:2). Christ was chosen before Creation (1 Peter 1:20). He was the Lamb that was slain from the creation of the world (Rev 13:8). The only other place the noun *prognosis* is used is Acts 2:23 and it also refers to the crucifixion of Christ.

Calvinism has connected *foreknowledge, predestination,* and *election* in a way Scripture does not. Calvinism teaches that God in His foreknowledge has chosen or decreed that some people are to be saved and some to be lost and there is not a thing in the world you can do about it. If you have been chosen to be saved you will be.

Wesleyan-Arminianism does not make these same connections. Wesley objected that Calvin's doctrine was no gospel, but called this teaching "horrible decrees."[1] God does foreknow everything, but he does not determine everything that will happen. He does determine (predestine) certain things. For instance, those who know him are predestined to be conformed to the

---

[1] This is actually Calvin's word in his *Institutes of the Christian Religion*, 3.23.7. Literally Calvin wrote, "Decretum quidem horribile, fateor." Wesley preached against "the horrible decree" [Letter to James Hutton, 30 April, 1739].

image of his son (Rom 8:29). And election is conditioned upon persevering faith, for as Jesus said, "He who stands firm to the end will be saved" (Matthew 10:22; 2 Peter 1:10).

Omnipotence - "I know that you can do all things; no plan of yours can be thwarted" (Job 42:2). "With God all things are possible" (Matt 19:26). God can do anything consistent with His nature. He cannot sin (2 Tim 2:13) nor lie (Heb 6:17-18; Titus 1:2).

Perfection - "As for God, his way is perfect" (Psalm 18:30). (For another use of the term "perfection," see page 61).

    1B. Communicable Attributes - qualities God imparts, in some measure, to man

Personhood - While God is invisible, he is not merely a force, but a person. God has a name. New Age teaching reduces God to energy. God speaks as "I"; he is not an "it." God is not nameless energy or an abstract idea. We are persons in his image.

Holiness - "Be holy because I, the Lord your God, am holy" (Lev 19:2). God is holy and is the source of our holiness.

    Holy as thee, O Lord is none!
        Thy holiness is all thy own;
    A drop of that unbounded sea
        Is ours, a drop derived from thee.

    And when thy purity we share,
        Thy only glory we declare;
    And humbled into nothing, own
        Holy and pure is God alone.

    [Charles Wesley, *Bicentennial Works of John Wesley*, Abingdon, 1983, 7:380].

For more on the subject of holiness as awe, see page 57.

Truth - "Let God be true and every man a liar" (Rom 3:4). God is true even if he contradicts all the teachings of men; however, God wants us also to speak the truth in love.

Love - "God is love" (1 John 4:16). This implies affection, good will, and understanding. God does have feelings; he is not stoic. God's love is demonstrated foremost through his Son. "This is love: not that we loved God, but that he loved us and send his Son as an atoning sacrifice for our sins" (1 John 4:10).

Righteousness - "Will not the Judge of all the earth do right?" (Gen 18:25).

Justice - "All his ways are just. A faithful God who does no wrong, upright and just is he" (Deut 32:4). Scripture reveals that God did not create evil, but that he will deal with it. "When we despair over our inevitable human condition, we lay an implicit charge against the justice of God" (Oden, *Systematic Theology*, 1:107).

Goodness - "How great is your goodness" (Psalm 31:19). "No good thing does he withhold from those whose walk is blameless" (Psalm 84:11).

Faithfulness - "God is faithful" (1 Cor 10:13).

Wisdom - "If any of you lacks wisdom, he should ask God" (James 1:5).

Graciousness - "For the grace of God that brings salvation has appeared to all men" (Titus 2:11).

Mercifulness - "God who is rich in mercy" (Eph 2:4). Grace means we get what we do not deserve; mercy means we do not get what we do deserve. "Let us then approach the throne of grace with confidence, so that we may receive mercy and find grace to help us in our time of need" (Heb 4:16).

Longsuffering - "He is patient with you, not wanting anyone to perish, but everyone to come to repentance" (2 Peter 3:9).

2. The Work of God

In this section we are going to deal with God's work in creation, preservation and providence. We have already addressed God's work in revelation. Under our discussion, beginning on page 26, we will consider God's work in redemption through Jesus Christ.

2A. Creation

God the Father created (Gen 1:1).

God the Son created (Col 1:16).

God the Spirit created (Gen 1:2, Psalm 104:30).

The purpose of creation was to declare God's glory (Psalm 19:1; Isa 43:7; Rev 4:11).

2B. Preservation

God has sustained and maintained what he created. "In him we live and move and have our being" (Acts 17:28). In Christ "all things hold together" (Col 1:17). Christ sustains all things by his powerful word (Heb 1:3).

2C. Providence

This word, although not used in Scripture, means "foresight." The concept of providence is taught in Romans 8:28, "God works together all things for our good."

In his providence, God permits, restrains or prevents certain acts, overrules certain acts, and prevents certain acts.

Miracles are considered special providence. God performs miracles to show that he is alive and willing to intervene in human history. God is able to transcend the very order he created. He did not lock himself out of his own creation.

For Further Reading:

Lewis, C. S. *Miracles*. New York: MacMillan, 1947.

Oden, Thomas C. *The Living God: Systematic Theology: Volume One*. San Francisco: Harper and Row, 1987.

Tozer, A. W. *The Knowledge of the Holy*. New York: Harper and Row, 1961.

Chapter Three

The Doctrine of Christ

1. The Person of Christ

1A. His Pre-incarnate Existence

"Before Abraham was born, I am!" (John 8:58). Abraham lived around two thousand years before the Incarnation. According to John 17:5, Christ existed with the Father before the creation of the world. According to Colossians 1:16, Christ created all things.

Did Christ have a beginning? If he is a created being he did have a beginning point; if he is the Creator he did *not* have a beginning. According to Hebrews 1, the angels are the highest created order and the angels worshiped Christ at his Incarnation. If Christ was a created being, this would amount to idolatry. Therefore, we conclude that Christ, as the Creator God, did not have a beginning point. This is the teaching of John 1:1-2. Only Christ existed before he was conceived.

1B. The Incarnation

If Christ was alive and active prior to his Incarnation, then the Incarnation does not mark the beginning of his existence, but it describes a humbling and a limitation of Christ.

The word *incarnation* is from Latin meaning "in flesh." At a point in time, the second person of the Godhead took on a human body. He is said to be the same because he has always been deity; he has not always been humanity. "The Word became flesh and made his dwelling among us" (John 1:14). God sent "his own Son in the likeness of sinful man to be a sin offering" (Rom 8:3).

He "who being in very nature God" became "made in human likeness" (Phil 2:6-7). "For in Christ all the fullness of the Deity lives in bodily form" (Col 2:9). "He had to be made like his brothers in every way" (Heb 2:17). "Therefore, when Christ came into the world, he said: Sacrifice and offering you did not desire, but a body you prepared for me" (Heb 10:5).

Philippians 2:5-8 describes the cost of the Incarnation. It involved condescension and humiliation. In v 7 "made himself nothing" literally is "he emptied himself." Of what did he empty himself? In the great hymn "And Can It Be" Charles Wesley overstates the point by saying, "Emptied himself of all but love." More accurately Christ left behind his heavenly glory, but not his deity (see John 17:5).

- There was a change in form - his appearance was like a man
- There was a change in position - he became a servant
- There was no change in nature - he is still God

The Incarnation was not terminated when Christ ascended. He is forever the God-man. He has become a priest forever (Heb 6:20).

1C. The Virgin Birth - the means of the Incarnation

Although Genesis 3:15 promised that the seed of a woman would deliver, Isaiah 7:14 is the first use of "virgin." The Hebrew word *almah* is not precise, although never used of married women. The Greek translation of the Old Testament (Septuagint) uses *parthenos*, which is not ambiguous; it can only mean "virgin." When Matthew quotes this verse in Matthew 1:23, it is *parthenos*.

It is also used by Luke the physician in Luke 1:34-35. Note that it is more precise to speak of the virgin conception. It was the conception, not the birth of Jesus which was miraculous.

✓Interview Question: What do you believe about the virgin birth of Jesus Christ?

1D. The Two Natures of Christ

Christ is fully God and fully man. He is one person with two natures. This truth has been confused by several heretical teachings which tend either to separate Christ into two persons or unite his two natures into one.

It is not necessary for salvation to have a technical grasp of theology, but it is heretical when theologians deny either his humanity or deity and it is important for the propagation of the faith that the truth be taught. If either nature of Christ is overemphasized, in time, error will develop.

2. The Humanity of Christ

He was not partially or occasionally human. He was fully human, yet without defect or sin. He was the second man and the last Adam (1 Cor 15:45-47). The most decisive proof of his humanity is that he died. Death came through a man, and the resurrection of the dead comes also through a man (1 Cor 15:21).

"The man Christ Jesus" is our only mediator (1 Tim 2:5). He shared in our humanity (Heb 2:14-18; 4:15-16).

Humanity was honored in the incarnation. Martin Luther preached that, "The devil came close to us; but he did not come so close as to assume our nature ... . He nevertheless did not become man and did not come so close to us as did God's Son, who became our flesh and blood."

3. The Deity of Christ

3A. Divine Titles Ascribed to Christ

3A1. Jesus calls himself "I am" in John 8:58. This is based on Exod 3:14, "I am because I am." The name "Yahweh" (or Jehovah) is based upon this verb "to be." Old Testament passages which refer to Yahweh are quoted in the NT and applied to Christ: Isa 40:3; Matt 3:3; Joel 2:32; Rom 10:13.

3A2. Jesus is called "Lord" (*kurios*) in Acts 10:36.

3A3. Jesus is called God:

"In the beginning was the Word . . . and the Word was God" (John 1:1). "Christ, who is God over all, forever praised" (Rom 9:5). "Our great God and Savior, Jesus Christ" (Titus 2:13). "But about the Son he says, 'Your throne, O God, will last for ever and ever'" (Heb 1:8). "Even in his Son Jesus Christ. He is the true God and eternal life" (1 John 5:20). Jesus Christ is established as the subject in Revelation 1:5. In v 8 he speaks directly, "'I am the Alpha and the Omega,' says the Lord God."

3A4. The term "Emmanuel" means "God with us" (Matt 1:23).

3B. Divine Attributes Ascribed to Christ:

Eternity - Isa 9:6; Rev 1:8, 17
Omnipresence - Matt 18:20; 28:20
Omniscience - John 2:24-25; 6:64; Rev 2:23
Omnipotence - Matt 28:18; Rev 1:8

3C. Divine Works Ascribed to Christ:

Creation - Col 1:16-17; Heb 1:2
Preservation - Col 1:17
Forgiveness of sins - Matt 9:2
Raising the dead - John 5:28-29
Final judgment - 2 Cor 5:10

3D. Divine Worship Paid to Christ: Matt 14:33

✓ Interview Question: What is your conviction about the deity of Christ?

4. The Work of Christ

The work of Christ in creation and in preservation have already been noted.

4A. Revelation

The agnostic claims we cannot know what God is like. Christ came to reveal God. Christ "has made him known" (John 1:18). "When a man believes in me, he does not believe in me only, but in the one who sent me. When he looks at me, he sees the one who sent me" (John 12:44-45). "Anyone who has seen me has seen the Father (John 14:8-11). "He is the image of the invisible God" (Col 1:15). The Son is the exact representation of God (Heb 1:3).

4B. Salvation

He came to save his people from their sins (Matt 1:21). He is the Lamb of God who takes away the sin of the world (John 1:29). Christ is the great teacher, example, and philosopher, but we would be unable to follow his example or obey his teachings if it were not for his salvation. He came to die that we might have spiritual life. Paul declares that the death, burial, and resurrection of Christ are "of first importance" (1 Cor 15:3).

4B1. His Substitutionary Death

"The Lord has laid on him the iniquity of us all" (Isa 53:4-6). He "gave his life as a ransom for many" (Matt 20:28). "One died for all" (1 Cor 5:14). "God made him who had no sin to be a sin offering for us" (1 Cor 5:21).

4B2. His Resurrection

"If Christ has not been raised, our preaching is useless and so is your faith .... And if Christ has not been raised, your faith is futile; you are still in your sins. Then those also who have fallen asleep in Christ are lost" (1 Cor 15:12-19).

The resurrection is not only celebrated at Easter, but each Sunday service provides a continuing testimony of the resurrection. The phrase "the first day of the week" was not found until the Gospel writers (Matt 28:1; Mark 16:2, 9; Luke 24:1; John 20:1, 9; Acts 20:7; 1 Cor 16:2). The resurrection was accepted as the firstfruits of a general resurrection (1 Cor 15:20; Col 1:18).

✓ Interview Question: What do you believe about the bodily resurrection of Christ?

4C. His Session

Jesus appeared on earth for forty days after his resurrection. Then he ascended back to heaven (Acts 1:9-11). "He who descended is the very one who ascended higher than all the heavens" (Eph 4:10).

The descent of the Spirit was the result of the ascent of Christ. He had promised to send the Holy Spirit (John 14:16-18; 16:7). "Exalted to the right hand of God, he has received from the Father the promised Holy Spirit and has poured out what you now see and hear" (Acts 2:33). The present work of Christ includes:

4C1. His Work of Intercession

"Christ Jesus ... is at the right hand of God and is also interceding for us" (Rom 8:34). "He always lives to intercede for them" (Heb 7:25). "We have one who speaks to the Father in our defense—Jesus Christ, the Righteous One" (1 John 2:1).

4C2. His Work of Preparation

"I am going there to prepare a place for you" (John 14:1).

4C3. His Work of Administration

"God has made this Jesus, whom you crucified, both Lord and Christ" (Acts 2:36). "That power is like the working of his mighty strength, which he exerted in Christ when he raised him from the dead and seated him at his right hand in the heavenly realms, far above all rule and authority, power and dominion, and every title that can be given, not only in the present age but also in the one to come. And God placed all things under his feet and appointed him to be head over everything for the church" (Eph 1:19-22). "To the only God our Savior be glory, majesty, power, and authority, through Jesus Christ our Lord, before all ages, now and forevermore!" (Jude 25). "The earth is the Lord's, and everything in it" (Psalm 24:1). "In putting everything under him, God left nothing that is not subject to him. Yet at present we do not see everything subject to him" (Heb 2:8).

4D. His Second Advent (coming)
The return of Christ will:

4D1. Reveal Christ's glory

"Look he is coming with the clouds, and every eye will see him, even those who pierced him; and all the peoples of the earth will mourn because of him" (Rev 1:7). "At the name of Jesus every knee should bow, in heaven and on earth and under the earth, and every tongue confess that Jesus Christ is Lord, to the glory of God the Father" (Phil 2:10-11).

4D2. Bring the work of salvation to completion

"He will appear a second time, not to bear sin, but to bring salvation to those who are waiting for him" (Heb 9:28).

4D3. Overthrow the world system

"And then the lawless one will be revealed, whom the Lord Jesus will overthrow with the breath of his mouth and destroy by the splendor of his coming" (2 Thess 2:8).

4D4. Establish a new heaven and earth

"But in keeping with his promise we are looking forward to a new heaven and a new earth, the home of righteousness" (2 Peter 3:13).

4D5. Raise the dead

"A time is coming when all who are in their graves will hear his voice and come out—those who have done good will rise to live, and those who have done evil will rise to be condemned" (John 5:28-29). "For the Lord himself will come down from heaven, with a loud command, with the voice of the archangel and with the trumpet call of God, and the dead in Christ will rise first" (1 Thess 4:16).

4D6. Judge the world

"For the Son of Man is going to come in his Father's glory with his angels, and then he will reward each person according to what he has done" (Matt 16:27; see also Matt 25:31-46). "Moreover, the Father judges no one, but has entrusted all judgment to the Son" (John 5:22). "For he has set a day when he will judge the world with justice by the man he has appointed. He has given proof of this to all men by raising him from the dead" (Acts 17:31). "For we must all appear before the judgment seat of Christ, that each one may receive what is due him for the things done while in the body, whether good or bad" (2 Cor 5:10).

✓Interview Question: What do you believe about the second coming of Christ?

For Further Reading:

Oden, Thomas C. *The Word of Life: Systematic Theology: Volume Two*. San Francisco: Harper and Row, 1989.

Wiley, H. Orton. *Christian Theology: Volume Two*. Kansas City: Beacon Hill, 1952, pp. 143-216.

Chapter Four

The Doctrine of the Holy Spirit

1. His Personality

The Holy Spirit is referred to by personal pronouns. The Greek word for "Spirit" is *pneuma* which is a neuter noun, yet the masculine pronoun is used of the Spirit in John 14:26; 15:26; 16:7. In other references, the pronoun "it" is used because in those cases the rules of grammar demand that the noun and pronoun agree.

In 1 John 2:1 Jesus is himself called a *parakletos*. In John 14:16-18 Jesus promises another *parakletos*, the Holy Spirit. In Greek there are two words for "another." One is another of a different kind (*heteros*) and the second is *allos*, another of the same kind. This second word is used in John 14. Jesus promises another paraclete just like himself. If Jesus is a person, so the Holy Spirit must also be a person. Therefore, the Holy Spirit should not be referred to as "it."

He can speak, be vexed, grieved, pleased, teach, guide, console, intercede, testify, be tempted, lied against, blasphemed.

2. His Deity

2A. The Spirit Is Given Divine Names.

He is called "God" (Acts 5:3-4). By definition, only God can be blasphemed. Since we are warned against blaspheming the Holy Spirit (Matt 12:31; Mark 3:29), he must be God.

2B. The Spirit Is Described as Having Divine Attributes.

He is *omnipresent*. "Where can I go from your Spirit? Where can I flee from your presence?" (Psalm 139:7-10) He is *omniscient*. "The Spirit searches all things, even the deep things of God" (1 Cor 2:10-11). He is called the *eternal* Spirit (Heb 9:14).

2C. The Spirit Performs Divine Works

In *creation* "the Spirit of God was hovering over the waters" (Gen 1:2). "The Spirit of God has made me; the breath of the Almighty gives me life" (Job 33:4).

"Men spoke from God as they were carried along by the Holy Spirit" (2 Peter 1:21). This is *inspiration*, which according to 2 Timothy 3:16 means "God-breathed." Hebrews 3:7 cites Psalm 95:7-11, which was written by David. However, Hebrews never credits any citation to its human author (except 4:7). Hebrews 3:7 credits the Holy Spirit.

In *regeneration* we are born of the Spirit (John 3:5-6). This renewal is by the Holy Spirit (Titus 3:5).

Christ was made alive by the Spirit (1 Peter 3:18). In the *resurrection* the Spirit who raised Jesus from the dead will also give life to our mortal bodies.

3. His Ministry

The Holy Spirit is often referred to as the executive of the Godhead. He also has a unique role in our salvation. Salvation was planned by the Father and purchased by the Son, but it is provided through the Spirit.

3A. The Spirit awakens and convicts us. "When he comes, he will convict the world of guilt in regard to sin and righteousness and judgment" (John 16:8-11).

3B. The Spirit enables us to repent. "God granted even the Gentiles repentance unto life" (Acts 11:18; see also 5:31). "God will grant them repentance" (2 Tim 2:25).

3C. The Spirit enables us to believe. The Spirit draws us to God (John 6:44, 65). Faith comes from hearing the Word (Rom 10:17). Faith is the gift of God (Eph 2:8).

3D. The Spirit creates new life. "I will give you a new heart and put a new spirit in you . . . And I will put my spirit in you and move you to follow my decrees and be careful to keep my laws" (Ezek 36:26-27). The new birth is the birth of the Spirit (John 3:5-8). This new life is the cleansing of all acquired pollution and renewal by the Holy Spirit

(Titus 3:5). Everyone who is born again has the Holy Spirit (Rom 8:9).

3E. The Spirit brings assurance. "The Spirit himself testifies with our spirit that we are God's children" (Rom 8:16). "Because you are sons, God sent the Spirit of his Son into our hearts, the Spirit who calls out, Abba, Father" (Gal 4:6). "Having believed, you were marked in him with a seal, the promised Holy Spirit, who is a deposit guaranteeing our inheritance" (Eph 1:13-14; see also 4:30).

3F. The Spirit teaches us and leads us. "When he, the Spirit of truth, comes, he will guide you into all truth" (John 16:13). "Those who are led by the Spirit of God are the sons of God (Rom 8:14).

3G. The Spirit produces the fruit of Galatians 5:19-23.

3G1. Toward God - love, joy, peace

3G2. Toward others - patience, kindness, goodness

3G3. In ourselves - faithfulness, gentleness, self-control

3H. The Spirit leads us on unto Christian perfection. "Let us be led on unto perfection" (literal translation of Heb 6:1). Christ loved the church and gave himself for her to make her holy, cleansing her by the washing with water through the word, and to present her to himself as a radiant church, without stain or wrinkle or any other blemish, but holy and blameless" (Eph 5:25-27). This perfecting of the Church was provided for by Christ, but is facilitated by the Spirit.

3I. The gifts of the Spirit will be discussed under the section on the doctrine of the Church.

For Further Reading:

Hogue, Wilson T. *The Holy Spirit: A Study*. 1916. Reprint Edition. Salem, OH: Schmul Publishers, 1998.

Oden, Thomas C. *The Word of Life: Systematic Theology: Volume Three*. San Francisco: HarperCollins, 1992.

Chapter Five

The Doctrine of the Trinity

We have seen that Father, Son, and Spirit are all regarded as God in Scripture. Yet we have also read that God is one (Deut 6:4). The rationalist will reject what he cannot understand, but it should not come as a surprise that God is beyond our ability to understand. If the Bible is his self-disclosure, let us not reject his description of himself simply because he is different than us. The doctrine of the trinity is not irrational or illogical; it is above or beyond human reason. "All explanations of the Trinity are inadequate. We are talking about a revealed mystery, something that by its very nature, and by our very nature, cannot be figured out by our rational processes" [J. Kenneth Grider, *A Wesleyan-Holiness Theology*, Beacon Hill, 1994, p. 123]. Tozer argued, "The fact that it cannot be satisfactorily explained, instead of being against it, is in its favor. Such a truth had to be revealed; no one could have imagined it" [*Knowledge of the Holy*, p. 31].

Indications of the trinitarian nature of God: (Some of the following verses are debated as to their trinitarian nature. But historically these verses have been interpreted as indicative that God is a Trinity. We want to emphasize that we believe that the Bible *does teach* the doctrine of the Trinity, and that the Bible cannot be properly understood apart from this understanding. These verses are compatible with that doctrine).

Elohim, a common Hebrew name for God, is plural.
Gen 1:26 who are the "us" and "our"?
Gen 3:22 "us"; see also 11:5-7
Isa 6:3 the three "holy"s

Matt 3:16-17
Matt 28:19
John 14:16-17
1 Cor 12:4-6
2 Cor 13:14
Eph 4:4-6
1 Peter 1:2
1 Peter 3:18
1 John 5:4-7

The previous reflections indicate that God is a compound being. Christ is one person with two natures; God is three persons but one in essence.

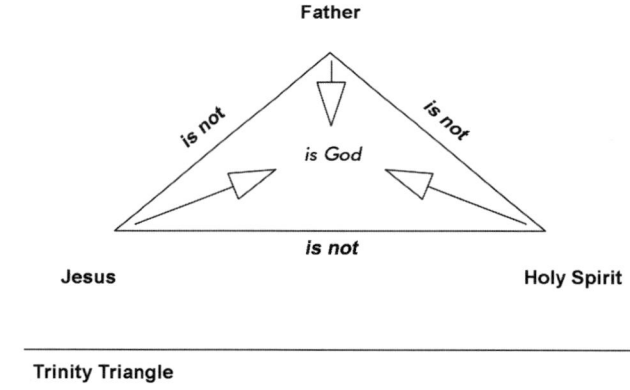

Trinity Triangle

✓ Interview Question: Explain your understanding of the relationships between the persons of the Godhead.

Chapter Six

The Doctrine of Mankind

Anthropology is from the word *anthropos*, the generic word for man—includes men and women and *logos*—a discourse. God is the center of theology, but man is the center of creation and salvation. Most theories about man are either too optimistic or too pessimistic. The human race is a magnificent ruin. Pascal said, "Man is the glory and scum of the universe."

1. The Creation of Man

Gen 1:26-28; 2:7, "Man *became* (from the verb 'to be') a living soul." Man did not evolve, he "became" by a direct act of God. Eve did not evolve. She was formed from Adam by God (Gen 2:21-23; 1 Cor 11:8). Man is distinct from animal life. We are not a higher form of animal; we are a little lower than God (*elohim* - Psalm 8:3-5).

We alone are made in God's image (Gen 1:26). Compare vv 24-25 where the creation is "each according to its kind" to v 26 where man "rules over nature." No suitable wife could be found for Adam from among creation (Gen 2:20; 1 Cor 15:39).

2. The Image of God

Theologians use the Latin term *Imago Dei* in their description of the Image of God in humanity. The *Imago Dei* is comprised of at least the following:

2A. Moral Image - righteousness and holiness; the capacity to love

2B. Natural Image - personality encompasses all that distinguishes human life from animal life:

    2B1. Intellectual power, self-consciousness, conscience, self-expression - language, literature, the arts, culture

    2B2. Spirituality - God is a spirit; He breathed into us the Spirit of life (the word for breath and spirit is the same word).

    2B3. Freedom of choice - man is held responsible for sin

    2B4. Immortality - if death is the result of sin, man was originally created immortal

2C. Political Image - man has dominion over the earth; he is to rule it under God.

The image of God in man has been greatly marred, but not completely lost. Our fall is total in the sense that we are affected in every area, yet man still has dignity and worth because of this fact. An adequate grasp of the Image of God leads us to the principle of the sanctity of all human life. For example, it is a sin to murder or take human life (Exod 20:13), because man is in the image of God. Murder, then, is an attack on the image of God.

Chapter Seven

The Doctrine of Sin

1. Sin Defined

The basic meaning of *sin* in the Old Testament means missing or transgressing God's absolute standard. This word is used in Judges 20:16, "each of whom could sling a stone at a hair and not *miss*." The basic New Testament meaning is also to miss the mark (*harmartia*), but there is more of an emphasis upon active rebellion.

A careful study of the Hebrew and Greek terms for sin will bear out these distinctions: sin as a state and as an act, sins of commission and sins of omission, unintentional and deliberate sin. For example, Numbers 15:22-31 makes a distinction between unintentional and defiant sin.

Sin is rebellion against God's sovereignty. Sin is autonomy or the setting up of ourselves as gods. The essence of sin is unbelief, pride (self-centeredness), disobedience, sensuality (self-gratification).

Greek Synonyms for Sin

adikea - wrongdoing, unrighteousness, injustice
hamartia – the most universal of all terms, meaning to miss the mark
parabasis - overstepping, transgression, disobedience
parakoe - failure to hear, carelessness, disobedience
paraptoma - trespass, false step, oversight, error, mistake (unintentional)
anomia - lawlessness, iniquity
asebeia - godlessness
agnoema - falling short, error, ignorance

hettema - defect, loss
aition - fault, crime
poneria - evil, wicked
apeitheia - disobedience, unbelief

The Hebrew language has at least eleven words for sin that correspond roughly to the Greek words. However, one Hebrew word refers to the burden and travail of sin (*amal*). This emphasis is absent in the New Testament; instead the emphasis is upon our toil for the cause of Christ. *Maal* is a breach or betrayal of trust, unfaithfulness. *Aven* means vanity or nothingness.

Because there are degrees and types of sin, there are various definitions of sin.

Sin is not believing in Christ (John 16:9).
Sin is suppression of the truth (Rom 1:18).
Sin is defiance against God's law (Rom 8:7).
Sin is whatever does not come from faith (Rom 14:23).
Sin is lawlessness (1 John 3:4).
Sin is refusal to do good (James 4:17).

Roman Catholics distinguish between *venial* and *mortal* sin. A sin may be willful, but considered *venial* if it is a small matter. "A sin can be venial in two ways: (1) when the evil done is not seriously wrong; (2) when the evil done is seriously wrong, but the sinner sincerely believes it is only slightly wrong or does not give full consent to it" [John Francis Noll, *Father Smith Instructs Jackson*, Lester J. Fallon, ed, Our Sunday Visitor Press, 1947, p. 76].

The problem with this rationale is that "little" sins often open the door to "big" sins. Roman Catholic theology also teaches there are seven deadly sins. They are called "capital sins" not because they are the worst sins, but because they are the chief reasons why men commit sin. The "seven deadly sins" are pride, covetousness, lust, anger, gluttony, envy, sloth.

John Wesley distinguished between willful sins and unintentional sins. He defined a sin, *properly so called*, as a "voluntary transgression of a known law of God" [*Works*, 10:394]. Other systems tend to make little distinction between these issues, preferring to emphasize that we all sin daily because we are human or finite. This discounts the possibility of deliverance from sin. 1 John 3:4-10 teaches that no one who is born of God will continue to sin. Wesley taught in *A Plain Account of Christian Perfection*,

(1.) Every one may mistake as long as he lives. (2.) A mistake in opinion may occasion a mistake in practice. (3.) Every such mistake is a transgression of the perfect law. Therefore, (4.) Every such mistake, were it not for the blood of atonement, would expose to eternal damnation. (5.) It follows, that the most perfect have continual need of the merits of Christ, even for their actual transgressions, and may say for themselves, as well as for their brethren, 'Forgive us our trespasses.'

This easily accounts for what might otherwise seem to be utterly unaccountable; namely, that those who are not offended when we speak of the highest degree of love, yet will not hear of living without sin. The reason is, they know all men are liable to mistake, and that in practice as well as in judgment. But they do not know, or do not observe, that this is not sin, if love is the sole principle of action.

In what sense do Christians not sin? This is established in 1 John 3:4—we are not lawless or rebellious. In Wesley's *Plain Account* is also found his famous explanation that "Not only sin, properly so called, (that is, a voluntary transgression of a known law,) but sin, improperly so called, (that is, an involuntary transgression of a divine law, known or unknown,) needs the atoning blood."

Thus, while Wesley agreed with the Calvinistic understanding of original sin, he believed that through prevenient grace involuntary sins or sins of ignorance were not imputed against us. Therefore, he wrote

Nothing is sin, strictly speaking, but a voluntary transgression of a known law of God. Therefore, every voluntary breach of the law of love is sin; and nothing else, if we speak properly. To strain the matter farther is only to make way for Calvinism. There may be ten thousand wandering thoughts and forgetful intervals without any breach of love, though not without transgressing the Adamic law. But Calvinists would fain confound these together. Let love fill your heart, and it is enough [Letter to Elizabeth Bennis, 16 June, 1772].

2. The Fall of Man

Adam and Eve were created without sin (Gen 2:25) and in God's image (Gen 1:26). Adam was commanded not to eat from the tree of the knowledge of good and evil (Gen 2:17). This was before Eve was created (Gen 2:21). Therefore, the tempter went to Eve who was the first to sin (1 Tim 2:13-14). She rebelled against her husband and against God. Adam, however, was held responsible as the head (1 Cor 15:22).

Results of the Fall

2A. Alienation - Adam and Eve hid (Gen 3:8)

2B. The moral image of God was lost, the natural image marred, and the political image imperiled.

2C. The whole earth was cursed (3:16-19; Rom 8:20-22)

2D. Death (Rom 5:12-18)

2E. Depravity - we are corrupt. The depravity is total, affecting the entire being of man.

    1). The affections are alienated

    2). The intellect is darkened

    3). The will is perverted [H. Orton Wiley, *Christian Theology*, 2:128-9].

    4). We are deprived of all that is good (Rom 7:18). There was a total loss of original righteousness.

    5). We are inclined to evil continually (Gen 6:5). James Arminius taught that while we did not lose our will, but we lost the power to will any good thing. [*The Writings of James Arminius,* James Nichols and W. R. Bagnall, eds, Baker, 1956, 1:252, 526; 3:196]. John Wesley preached, "Such is the freedom of his will - free only to evil" ["The Spirit of Bondage and of Adoption," Sermon #9, 2.7-8].

3. Total Depravity

3A. Scriptural Evidences for Total Depravity

Psalm 51:5, Jer 17:9, Matt 7:11, Rom 3:10-18, Eph 2:3, Eph 4:22, James 4:1-2, 2 Peter 1:4.

Total depravity is the condition which results from original sin. "Original sin refers to a state of sin in us due to that original act of sin on Adam's part" [Grider, *A Wesleyan-Holiness Theology*, p. 277]. The original act of sin on Adam's part has been imputed to us, since we are connected to Adam as the federal head of our race. By *federal head* we mean what Wesley meant in Volume Nine of his *Works* where he wrote that Adam was a representative of our race, by which all mankind fell into "sorrow, pain, and death, both spiritual and temporal" [See pages 332-34; "The Spirit of Bondage and Adoption,"

2.7]. Gen 5:3 says Adam "had a son in his own likeness, in his own image." We, too, inherit his sinful tendency. This is called "original sin." (For more on Federal Headship, see Wiley, *Christian Theology,* 2:133; On original sin, see 2:96-140).

G. K. Chesterton called original sin the only empirically verifiable Christian doctrine, by which he meant the condition of sin can be observed every day in society. Wesley preached that anyone who denied original sin are but heathens still. He claimed this as "the first grand distinguishing point between heathenism and Christianity" ["Original Sin," 3.1].

In Wesley's 272 page treatise, "The Doctrine of Original Sin," he declared without this doctrine "the Christian system falls at once" [*Works*, 9:194]. Kenneth Collins explained "a weak doctrine of original sin could only result in an equally weak doctrine of the new birth. For if the extensiveness of the problem was relinquished or soft-pedaled, the radical nature of the solution would be lost as well" [*Wesley on Salvation*, p. 22].

It is this condition of total depravity that makes the new birth necessary. Since we were born in sin, we must be born again. All have sinned (Rom 3:23) because all are sinners. We have not only inherited depravity, but we acquire depravity by wrong choices. We stand guilty before God because of our sins. The wages of sin is death (Rom 6:23). The sinner is dead in sin (Eph 2:1). The sinner faces the second death, eternal separation from God (Rev 2:11; 20:14; 21:8).

If we cannot help but sin, why does God hold us guilty and punish us? Although we are fallen, we still have a consciousness of right and wrong. Although we have a bias toward sin and our tendency is to choose wrong, through prevenient grace we are given the possibility of choosing right and we are held responsible for our choices.

3B. Misconceptions Concerning Total Depravity

1. "This depravity must not, however, be regarded as a physical entity or any other form of essential existence added to man's nature" [Wiley, 2:119].

2. It does not mean that every man is as thoroughly depraved as he can possibly become. Depravity is extensive, affecting the entire being of man, but not necessarily intensive.

3. It does not mean that every sinner will indulge in every form of sin.

4. It does not mean that the sinner has no innate knowledge of the will of God or conscience (Rom 2:15).

5. It does not mean that sinful man is incapable of good acts toward his fellow man. It does mean that a sinner's good works are not good enough, however, since they do not arise from faith in Jesus Christ.

For Further Reading:

Collins, Kenneth J. *Wesley on Salvation*. Grand Rapids: Francis Asbury Press, 1989.

Grider, J. Kenneth. *A Wesleyan-Arminian Theology*. Kansas City: Beacon Hill, 1994. Chapter 10.

Wesley, John. "The Spirit of Bondage and of Adoption." Sermon # 9. "Original Sin." Sermon #44. "The Doctrine of Original Sin," in *Works*, Volume 9.

Wiley, H. Orton. *Christian Theology*. Kansas City: Beacon Hill, 1952. Chapters 18-19 in Volume 2.

Chapter Eight

Doctrine of The Atonement

The atonement is the heart of the Gospel. "May I never boast except in the cross of our Lord Jesus Christ" (Gal 6:14).

The Hebrew word *kaphar* means to cover. It is used in Gen 6:14 to cover over with pitch. Yom Kippur is the Day of Atonement. "Atonement" is found only once in the KJV, at Rom 5:11. However, three Greek words carry the basic meaning of atonement:

katallasso - to reconcile
hilaskomai - to propitiate; to turn away the anger of God
lutroo - to redeem or ransom

These three words correspond to three Atonement themes:

legal - propitiation and justification
commercial - redemption
relational - reconciliation

1. The Necessity of the Atonement

The doctrine of total depravity teaches that man can do nothing to save himself. We are under the wrath of God. There are over 580 references to the wrath of God in the Old Testament. Over twenty Hebrew words are used to express this wrath. Sin is rebellion against God. "The sinful mind is hostile to God. It does not submit to God's law, nor can it do so" (Rom 8:7). "God is angry with the wicked every day" (Psalm 7:11). We must flee the wrath to come (Matt 3:7). We need propitiation.

We are alienated from God. God cannot look with favor upon sin. "Your eyes are too pure to look on evil; you cannot tolerate wrong" (Hab 1:13). We need reconciliation.

We are bound by our sinful nature and are under the sentence of death because of our sins. To use commercial language, we need redemption. We owed a debt we could not pay. He paid a debt he did not owe.

If we are saved, God must provide atonement. We can assume that he would not have paid the supreme price of his Son if a lesser price would have paid for our sins. God was under no obligation to rescue us, but because of his love he chose to do so. However, he must save us in a plan consistent with his nature. How can he be both just and the one who justifies (Rom 3:26)? If God is sovereign, why could he not forgive our sin without any atonement? Since all have sinned, surely God will "grade on the curve." No, God said the penalty for sin was death (Gen 2:17; Rom 6:23). God must keep his word for he cannot lie (John 17:17; Rom 3:4; Titus 1:2; Heb 6:18). God is bound by his truthfulness and justice. Justice and holiness demand punishment. The demands of the law must be satisfied. Sin deserves punishment.

The atonement has two key elements—substitution and satisfaction. In some cases, particular theories exaggerate one aspect and omit the other. A proper view of the atonement takes into account the love of God and the wrath of God, the satisfaction of his law and moral government, victory over Satan, and reconciliation with God.

2. The Atonement as Substitution

The Bible teaches that Christ was our substitute (the Latin word is *vicar*): "He was pierced for our transgressions, he was crushed for our iniquities; the punishment that brought us peace was upon him, and by his wounds we are healed" (Isa 53:5). "to give his life a ransom for (*anti* – in place of) many" (Matt 20:28, Mk 10:45). "When we were still powerless, Christ died for (*huper* – in behalf of, for the sake of) the ungodly . . . But God demonstrates his own love for [to] us in this: While we were still sinners, Christ died for (*huper* – in behalf of, for the sake of) us" (Rom 5:6-8).

Only Christ could qualify as our substitute because he alone is fully human, yet sinless. The Incarnation was necessary for this reason. "God made him who had no sin to be sin for us, so that in him we might become the righteousness of God" (2 Cor 5:21). However, the Incarnation limited Christ to becoming a substitute for the human race. No salvation is provided for fallen angels.

Since Christ is also God, his life was of infinite value. The payment of Christ was sufficient, not an exact equivalent. He overpaid and therefore salvation by human works is an insult. The emphasis should not be upon the quantity of suffering, but the quality of the One suffering.

3. The Atonement as Satisfaction

James Arminius taught that God "rendered satisfaction to *his Love for Justice and to his Hatred against sin*, when he imposed on his Son the office of Mediator by the shedding of his blood and by the suffering of death; and he was unwilling to admit him as the Intercessor for sinners except when sprinkled with his own blood in which he might be made the propitiation for sins ... . In this respect also it may with propriety be said, that God rendered satisfaction to himself, and appeased himself in "the Son of his love" ["Public Disputations," *Works*, 2:221-222].

The blood of Jesus:

3A. Satisfies the justice of God. "He shall see the travail of his soul and be satisfied. By his knowledge my righteous servant shall justify many" (Isa 53:11). Sometimes his death is viewed as a demonstration of God's love, but not the satisfaction of God's law. It is both.

3B. Dismisses the claim of Satan. "You were bought at a price" (1 Cor 7:23), should not be interpreted to mean that we were ransomed from Satan. We were released from the slavery of sin. God did not owe the devil anything and does not do business with him. "Satisfaction is to be made, not to the jailer, but to him whose law has been violated" [Richard Watson, *Theological Institutes*, 2:126].

4. The Extent of the Atonement

Calvinists and Arminians debate whether Christ intended to atone for the sins of the whole world or only for the elect. Calvin himself taught that while Christ dies for all, he intercedes only for the elect. It is the intercession of Christ which makes his atonement effectual and his intercession is based upon the decree of election. While the atonement is sufficient to save all, it is efficient only to save the elect. The hope of salvation is thus moved from a universal atonement to a sovereign decree. Arminians contend that the provision is for all, but it is effectual only for those who believe.

Scriptures which teach the universal atonement: John 1:29, 3:16; Rom 5:17-21, 2 Cor 5:14-19, 1 Tim 2:6, Titus 2:11, Heb 2:9, 2 Peter 3:9, 1 John 2:2.

✓Interview Question: What do you believe about the death of Christ as an atonement for our sins?

Chapter Nine

The Doctrine of Salvation

The doctrine of sin reveals our need of salvation. The doctrine of atonement reveals God's provision for salvation.

Salvation is by grace alone. We are saved by grace through faith (Eph 2:8-9). Thus, we can espouse the Reformer's formula: We are saved by grace alone, through faith alone, in Christ alone. By grace we mean undeserved, upwelling, abundant divine favor exercised in our behalf and for our benefit. While grace flows from God's nature, it impacts us in various ways according to our specific need. Thus we can speak of common grace (Matt 5:45), prevenient grace, justifying grace, and sanctifying or perfecting grace.

The doctrine of grace can be abused, namely Bonhoeffer's reference to cheap grace. The doctrine of grace can also be misused to allow for carnal living and/or license. But Paul said the grace of God teaches us to live upright, godly, self controlled lives and to deny ungodliness and worldly passions (Titus 2:11-15).

By grace we also mean the sovereign, beneficence of God by which he not only calls humans to salvation, but also by which he enables us to respond to his call, and which we will now begin to discuss.

1. The Divine Initiative

1A. Prevenient/Preliminary Grace

Christ, the true light, gives light to every man (John 1:9). "The grace of God that brings salvation has appeared to all men" (Titus 2:11). The gift of grace, described in Ephesians 2:8 includes preceding or prevenient grace.

Prevenient comes from two Latin words, *prae* (before) and *venire* (to come). Preventing or prevenient grace is the grace of God which precedes or comes before human action. Wesley understood that the grace of God enables a sinner to repent and believe. He calls this grace "preventing grace." He said

> salvation begins with what is usually termed (and very properly) "preventing grace;" including the first wish to please God, the first dawn of light concerning his will, and the first slight, transient conviction of having sinned against him. All these imply some tendency toward life, some degree of salvation, the beginning of deliverance from a blind, unfeeling heart, quite insensible of God and the things of God ["On Working Out Our Own Salvation," Sermon #85, 2.1].

Wesley also said that "preventing grace" included

> all the "drawings" of "the Father," the desires after God, which, if we yield to them, increase more and more; all that "light" wherewith the Son of God "enlighteneth everyone that cometh into the world," *showing* every man "to do justly, to love mercy, and to walk humbly with his God"; all the *convictions* which his Spirit from time to time works in every child of man. Although it is true the generality of men stifle them as soon as possible, and after a while forget, or at least deny, that ever they had them at all ["The Scripture Way of Salvation," Sermon #43, 1.2].

1B. The Gospel Call

The Gospel call is the drawing of the Spirit. Jesus said, "No one can come to me unless the Father who sent me draws him" (John 6:44). Yet all men are drawn (John 12:32). The call is stated in passages such as Isa 55 and Matt 11:28-30. While this call is stated in Scripture, the Church is also commissioned to go into all the world and declare the terms of salvation. The Holy Spirit usually draws sinners to Christ through the preaching of the gospel (Rom 10:14).

Calvinism teaches that a general or external call is to be preached universally, but that the call is effectual or inward only in the elect. The evangelist can issue a general call, but it will be irresistible only for those who are elect. This destroys the "good news" of the gospel for the reprobate or non-elect.

Actually this call is not irresistible. Jesus taught that "many are called, but few are chosen" (Matt 22:14). "Therefore, my brothers, be all the more eager to make your calling and election sure. For if you do these things you will never fall" (2 Peter 1:10).

Calvinists object that if God is sovereign, his call cannot be resisted. We affirm the sovereignty of God, but believe that God can choose to limit his power. The call is an invitation, not a conscription.

While Calvinism teaches that the call of God is irresistible and the election of God is unconditional, Peter teaches we must confirm both. Then he states a condition. For doing these things, you will by no means ever fall. The implication is that if we do not follow through on our commitment that we will fall. But what does it mean to fall? v 11 explains that those who do not fall away will be welcomed into heaven. The implication is that those who do fall away will not be welcomed into heaven.

1C. Conviction and Awakening

John 16:8-11 describes the convicting work of the Holy Spirit. We are convicted over sin and the ultimate sin is to deny Christ. We are convicted over our unrighteousness. Christ returned to heaven, but we are not fit for heaven. We are convicted over the coming judgment.

Evangelicalism today is plagued with an easy believing that cuts past conviction and repentance. Too often this "discount" approach only inoculates against the real thing.

Francis Schaeffer said if he had an hour to present the gospel to modern man, he would use 45 minutes to show the man his dilemma. "Then I'd take ten or fifteen minutes to preach the gospel .... I believe that much of our evangelism and personal work today is not clear simply because we are too anxious to get the answer without having a man realize the real cause of his sickness" [*Works*, 4:251].

This awareness that we are a sinner and have fallen far from God's original intention for us is often referred to as being "awakened." Wesley taught that a natural man neither feared nor loved God. An awakened sinner feared, but did not yet love God [*Notes* on 1 John 4:18].

An awakened sinner finds the pleasure of sin is gone. His concern is depicted in Romans 7:14-25. Although he purposes to improve his life, he discovered he is bound by sin.

In some theological systems the consciousness of sin and the concern over it is considered sufficient evidence that a person is born again. Martin Luther stated that a person is both justified and yet a sinner. Wesley used several phrases to differentiate between the awakened state and the new birth. He called the convicted sinner "the almost Christian." He described this as "the legal state" or "the faith of a servant." Wesley was convinced that many devout and earnest people never passed beyond this state. Please note that all "sons" are servants of God, but not all servants enjoy the benefits of sonship.

2. The Human Response

The only appropriate human response to God's provision of salvation, and thus the only condition for salvation, is obedient faith, which manifests itself in repentance of sin and trust in the substitutionary death of Jesus Christ.

2A. Repentance

What is the awakened sinner to do? He is called upon by Scripture to repent. Repentance is the first step in human response. Yet even our response is enabled by grace. Repentance is the gift of God.

"God granted even the Gentiles repentance unto life" (Acts 11:18). "God will grant them repentance leading them to a knowledge of the truth" (2 Tim 2:25).

However, we will have no inclination to repent until we are convicted. *Confession* means to agree with the charges brought by the Holy Spirit. It means that we plead guilty. Repentance is a change of mind about sin that results in a turning from sin.

We begin to feel a deep sorrow of heart for our sin. We deplore ourselves for having lived so foolishly. We thought we were wise, but begin to realize that in truth we have been a fool. We are grieved to recognize that we have trampled both the laws of God and the blood of his Son under foot.

Repentance is not false humility. Nor is repentance a matter of making excuses. It is not the fear of getting caught nor grief over the consequences of bad choices. Repentance is a radical change of heart. It is a deep remorse and regret over hurting others, condemnation for violating your own integrity, and most of all, sorrow over offending God. Repentance is a radical change of mind. Sin is not caused by our heredity or environment, our physiological temperament or the stars. To repent means we accept personal responsibility for our sin and have changed our way of thinking. We have made a commitment to the truth which produces a change in our conduct. It is a change of values in which we turn from the value system of the world and adopt the values taught by God's Word.

Repentance is a radical change of will in which we surrender control over our life and submit to the Lordship of Jesus Christ. "Repent! Turn away from all your offenses; then sin will not be your downfall. Rid yourselves of all the offenses you have committed, and get a new heart and a new spirit" (Ezek 18:30-31).

Paul distinguished between the sorrow of the world and godly sorrow which produces repentance. "See what this godly sorrow has produced in you: what earnestness, what eagerness to clear yourselves, what indignation, what alarm, what longing, what concern, what readiness to see justice done" (2 Cor 7:10-11).

Jesus preached repentance as a condition to salvation in at least nineteen passages. He declared, "Unless you repent, you too will all perish" (Luke 13:3).

The desire for forgiveness and acceptance by God grows stronger as our sorrow for sin deepens. We attempt to reform our life by leaving off the sins of the past and striving to obey God's commands. We try to turn away from idols and serve the living God. We pray for forgiveness and request mercy as we begin to honestly acknowledge all of the known sin that has been in our life.

See Thomas Oden, *Life in the Spirit: Systematic Theology, Volume Three.* San Francisco: HarperCollins, 1992. pp. 85-101.

2B. Faith

It is impossible to exercise saving faith until we have genuinely repented. Faith is also the gift of God (Eph 2:8; Phil 1:29). Yet we are commanded to believe.

Stages of Faith

> 2B1. Faith begins as an intellectual acceptance of the truth. Our faith must have content. Our faith is not in the power of faith.

Francis Schaeffer wrote about "pre-evangelism." We can no longer presume the sinner has a Christian framework of truth. A person cannot put faith in a Christ he knows nothing about [*Works,* 1:151-160].

Yet faith must go beyond mental ascent. The demons "believe" in the sense that they know certain truths to be true, yet they remain demons (James 2:19).

> 2B2. Faith also involves the consent of the will. There must be a deliberate decision to accept Christ as my substitute and trust solely in his atoning work.

But are we saved because we have determined that we have sufficiently believed? How do we know when we have sufficiently believed? This can easily degenerate into mental gymnastics and logical deductions. If "the heart is deceitful above all things" (Jer 17:9), it is not safe to make these assumptions.

> 2B3. Faith also includes assurance or confirmation that we are forgiven and accepted. This knowledge comes from an external source, the Holy Spirit, who brings an inner confidence.

Why do we say that faith is the only condition necessary for salvation? Properly understood, repentance is an act of faith. Faith cannot be separated from obedience. The Greek verb *pitho* which is often translated "trust," "having confidence," "assurance," or "being persuaded" is translated six times as "obey" in the KJV. Hebrews 3:18 said the Israelites did not enter into God's blessing because of disobedience. The very next verse says they did not enter in because of unbelief. Faith and obedience are two sides of the same coin.

Philip Melanchthon, early Lutheran theologian, said, "It is faith alone which saved, but the faith that saves is not alone."

Verses like Mark 1:15 command us to repent and believe. Why did Paul tell the jailer simply to "believe on the Lord Jesus Christ" (Acts 16:31)? Why did Peter preach to "repent and be baptized" (Acts 2:38) and not mention faith at all?

The New Testament prescribes faith, without any mention of repentance, 115 times. However, in other passages repentance is used to cover the whole process while faith is not mentioned (Luke 24:47; Acts 2:38; 3:19; 5:31). Jesus preached repentance as a condition to salvation at least 19 times. Sometimes "faith" includes repentance even if repentance is not specifically mentioned. Actually both constitute a single act; repentance is turning away from sin and faith is turning toward grace. Strictly speaking faith is the only condition of conversion, but repentance is a part of faith [Oden, *Systematic Theology*, 3:79-108].

3. The New Birth

When human beings respond to the divine initiative, God brings forth new life. The new birth is described by the use of several metaphors in the New Testament.

> 3A. Justification - we were under the wrath and judgment of God; through faith we trust in Christ as our propitiation.

Justification is a judicial act of God in which he declares on the basis of Christ's death that all the claims of the law are satisfied with respect to the sinner. We can only be justified by faith in Jesus Christ (Gal 2:16). Paul makes two statements which give both sides of this judicial act of God. "There is now no condemnation for those who are in Christ Jesus" (Rom 8:1). I am forgiven. The demands of the law have been satisfied. "Since we have been justified through faith, we have peace with God" (Rom 5:1). I am reconciled. I am brought near through the blood of Christ.

✓ Interview Question: What do you believe about justification by faith?

3B. Regeneration

God not only forgives my sins, he gives me a new nature—the righteousness of Christ. Justification is what God does *for* us; regeneration is what God does *in* us. *Regeneration* is related to the word "genesis" which means "beginning." "Regeneration" is a new beginning. It means to be born again by the Holy Spirit, to be born from above. It is the impartation of spiritual life.

1). It is divine generation (1 John 5:1).
2). It is divine creation (2 Cor 5:17).
3). It is spiritual resurrection (Eph 2:1; John 5:25).
4). It is participation in the divine nature (2 Peter 1:4).

This was promised in Ezek 36:25-27, "I will give you a new heart and put a new spirit in you; I will remove from you your heart of stone and give you a heart of flesh. And I will put my Spirit in you and move you to follow my decrees and be careful to keep my laws." All believers have the Holy Spirit (Rom 8:9) and there is no command in the New Testament for Christians to receive the baptism with the Holy Spirit. The command in Eph 5:18 is a present tense command to keep filled with the Spirit.

✓ Interview Question: What is your understanding of the indwelling of the Holy Spirit?

3C. Adoption

Adoption is that work of the Spirit by which we are received into the family of God. Adoption is a legal means by which a child not of the family can be taken into the family with full rights and privileges of that relationship. We who were created by God were disinherited by sin and had become aliens and outcasts. Yet through faith in Christ we are received into the family of God and given the privileges of sonship (Rom 8:15, 17, 23; Gal 4:7). We are no longer aliens, outcasts, disenfranchised. In Romans 8:15 the Holy Spirit is termed the "Spirit of adoption." Paul alone uses the analogy of adoption to describe salvation.

The Father-Son relationship is not described in the Old Testament. John writes, "<u>Now</u> we are the sons of God" (1 John 3:2). Rarely did anyone address God as father. Jesus scandalized his hearers by using this as his regular address. Abba is a term of intimacy—dear father.

Jewish slaves were never allowed to address their master as "father." Muslims object strongly to calling God our father, considering it blasphemy to say "my father." They also object to Jesus being called the "Son of God." They insist that God has no children and call themselves "servants of God."

The Holy Spirit pours the love of God into our hearts (Rom 5:5). This Spirit of adoption causes us to cry, Abba, Father. "Abba" is the Aramaic word for "father." It is followed by the Greek word *pater*. No matter what language we speak, we have the same father.

3D. The Witness of the Spirit

When a person is born again, he/she receives a direct internal witness of the Holy Spirit. In the New Testament, the witness of the Spirit is considered from several angles.

3D1. A Seal (2 Cor 1:22; Eph 1:13-14; 4:30)

According to 2 Cor 1:22 it is God who seals us and the Holy Spirit is the seal. All who truly believe are thus sealed and nowhere are believers encouraged to seek the seal of the Spirit as though it was a subsequent work of grace. Adam Clarke commented, "God has no child who is not a partaker of the Holy Ghost, and he who has this Spirit has God's *seal* that he belongs to the heavenly family" [*Commentary*, 5:434]. The purpose of a seal is to authenticate, protect, and denote ownership.

> 3D2. An earnest or down payment (Eph 1:13-14). The Greek word for earnest used in this passage, *arrabon,* is used today in modern Greek to refer to an engagement ring [Moulton and Milligan, *Vocabulary of the Greek New Testament*. 1930; rpt. Peabody, MA: Hendrickson, 1997, p 79]. This is a beautiful metaphorical expression of the relationship of the Holy Spirit to the church. The Spirit is Christ's "engagement promise" to his bride.

3D3. A testimony (Rom 8:16; Gal 4:6).

The *manner* how the divine testimony is manifested to the heart, I do not take upon me to explain. "Such knowledge is too wonderful and excellent for me: I cannot attain unto it." "The wind bloweth, and I hear the sound thereof;" but I cannot "tell how it cometh, or whither it goeth." As no one knoweth the things of a man, save the spirit of a man that is in him; so the *manner* of the things of God knoweth no one, save the Spirit of God. But the fact we know; namely, that the Spirit of God does give a believer such a testimony of his adoption that while it is present to the soul, he can no more doubt the reality of his sonship, than he can doubt of the shining of the sun, while he stands full blaze of his beams [John Wesley, "The Witness of the Spirit, I," Sermon #10, 1.12].

4. Christian Security

We believe the Bible teaches the security of the believer. However, "some persons confound ... assurance of present acceptance with an assurance of final salvation. The one is very distinct from the other. I find no authority for the last in the book of God" [Richard Watson, *Sermons*, 2:349]. Thus, we do not hold to the doctrine of unconditional eternal security.

Many who cling to the teaching of unconditional security have no confidence that they are accepted by God. The emphasis for Christian security should be placed upon assurance of our present relationship, not presumption about unconditional security for the future. Rom 8:31-39 promises security to the believer, but 8:15-16 also promises present assurance to the believer. Unless one has assurance that he/she is now born again, he/she should not presume on the eternal security of the believer.

The following scriptural warnings should be sufficient to alert the believer that his state of grace is not unconditional, but conditioned upon the continuation of the life of obedient faith.

The Conditional Security of the Believer

"If a righteous man turns from his righteousness and commits sin and does the same detestable things the wicked man does, will he live? None of the righteous things he has done will be remembered . . . he will die" (Ezek 18:24; see also v 26; 33:12-18).

"If you hold to my teaching, you are really my disciples; If anyone does not remain in me, he is like a branch that is ... thrown into the fire and burned" (John 8:31; 15:6).

"By this gospel you are saved, if you hold firmly to the word I preached to you. Otherwise, you have believed in vain" (1 Cor 15:2).

"Some will abandon the faith. ... Be diligent ... watch your life and doctrine closely. Persevere in them, because if you do, you will save both yourself and your hearers" (1 Tim 4:1; 15-16). "If we endure we will also reign with him" (2 Tim 2:12).

"It is impossible for those who have once been enlightened, who have tasted the heavenly gift, who have shared in the Holy Spirit, who have tasted the goodness of the word of God and the powers of the coming age, if they fall away, to be brought back to repentance while to their loss they are crucifying the Son of God all over again" (Heb 6:4-6).

"If we deliberately keep on sinning after we have received the knowledge of the truth, no sacrifice for sins is left, but only a fearful expectation of judgment and of raging fire that will consume the enemies of God" (Heb 10:26-29).

"If one of you should wander from the truth and someone should bring him back, remember this: Whoever turns a sinner from the error of his way will save him from death and cover over a multitude of sins" (James 5:19-20).

"Be all the more eager to make your calling and election sure. For if you do these things, you will never fall" (2 Peter 1:10-11). "If they have escaped the corruption of the world by knowing our Lord and Savior Jesus Christ and are again entangled in it and overcome, they are worse off at the end than they were at the beginning. It would have been better for them not to have known the way of righteousness, than to have known it and then to turn their backs on the sacred command that was passed on to them" (2 Peter 2:20-22).

"He who overcomes will not be hurt at all by the second death" (Rev 2:11). "He who overcomes ... I will never blot out his name from the book of life" (Rev 3:5).

For Further Reading:

Oden, Thomas C. *Life in the Spirit: Systematic Theology: Volume 3*. Chapter 3, "The Way of Repentance."
Wesley, John. "On Working Out Our Own Salvation," Sermon #85; "The Scripture Way of Salvation," Sermon #43; "The Witness of the Spirit, I and II," Sermons #10-11.

Chapter Ten

The Doctrine of Sanctification

Philip Watson summarized Wesley's teachings with this simple formula:

a. All men need to be saved.
b. All men can be saved.
c. All men can know they are saved.
d. All men can be saved to the uttermost.

[*The Message of the Wesleys: A Reader of Instruction and Devotion* 1964; Rpt, Zondervan, 1984, 35].

God can save completely or to the uttermost (Heb 7:25). This phrase means salvation is to the farthest extent, to the greatest degree, to the most distant point. Full salvation is not only freedom from the guilt, the bondage, and the power of sin, but cleansing from the pollution and nature of sin and ultimately deliverance from the very presence of sin. But how much of this complete salvation may be experienced in this life? "Now to him who is able to do immeasurably more than all we ask or imagine, according to his power that is at work with us" (Eph 3:20). While this verse does not give us a complete answer to this question directly, it does suggest that we should not limit the possibilities of grace.

The doctrine of sanctification begins with the doctrine of sin. Those who deny man's complete helplessness cannot teach correctly about sanctification. In the new birth, the bondage of sin is broken. Sin remains, but does not reign. Isaiah 53:5 promised that Christ would become the substitute for our transgression (outward sins) and our iniquities (inborn crookedness). Romans 6:6 teaches that the old life is crucified and also that the body of sin may be destroyed or abolished. This Greek word *katargeo* means to put away, to render inoperative, inactive or powerless. It is also used in 1 Cor 13:11 where we are to put childish ways behind us.

Sanctification in the Old Testament is based on the Hebrew word transliterated *kadosh* or *qodesh*. It carried three ideas:

1. Awe

Holiness meant brilliance or radiance when it represented the unique nature and awesome presence of God (Gen 28:17, Job 4:12-17, Isa 6:5). The holiness of God needs to be tied to the word "glory." We need to recover a sense of awe and reverence. The revelation of God's holiness is a traumatic experience. Rudolf Otto wrote in *The Idea of the Holy* [John W. Harvey, trans. Oxford, 1958] that when the human comes in contact with the divine it produces a sense of awe, majesty, vitality, otherness, fascination. And it also makes us uncomfortable.

2. Purity

This ethical emphasis becomes more prominent in the prophetic section of the Old Testament and in the New Testament. God is absolute purity (Hab 1:13, Jas 1:13). His wrath is his resistance to everything unholy. The Old Testament uses over 20 words a total of 580 times in reference to his wrath. But while he is repulsed by that which is unclean, he does not abandon us in our sinful condition. While his holiness cannot tolerate evil, yet his love embraces the sinner. Thus, we list love as an attribute of God, but not wrath because his wrath is temporary and his love is eternal (Isa 54:7-8; Hosea 14:4). His anger is holy; his love is holy. He is good all the time. His anger burns hot when we deliberately break his holy law, but his holy love provides a way out. I can understand his anger; I cannot comprehend his love. He is justified in his wrath, but his holy love is the highest expression of his holiness.

3. Transcendence or Consecration

Holiness meant separation. The context could mean something unapproachable because of danger, unapproachable because of excellence, or set aside for moral excellence and worship. Theologians have attempted to describe this separateness by explaining that God is "wholly other" (See Isa 40:25).

Sanctification is used most frequently to describe the state of consecration effected by the Levitical ritual. Of all the occurrences of the word *kadosh* (and its variant spellings) in the Old Testament, 20% occur in Leviticus. The largest section of holiness code in Leviticus (chapters 17-27) is given over largely to ceremonial and external regulations. It did not imply that the person or object became ethically or morally pure. It meant that they were set apart for holy use.

The tabernacle, anointing oil, incense, shewbread, the priest's clothing, holy days or seasons were all sanctified in this sense. Kings were anointed for leadership. Priests served in a holy function. Prophets spoke the Word of God. However, they were holy in function, not as a person. The prophets looked forward to a personal holiness under the new covenant which went beyond ceremonial holiness.

In the New Testament *hagiasmos* refers primarily to a moral condition. "The sacred no longer belongs to things, places or rites, but to the manifestations of life produced by the Spirit" [*The New International Dictionary of New Testament Theology*, 2:224-232].

1. Stages of Christian Sanctification

1A. *Initial sanctification* is closely related to regeneration.

When a person truly believed, he was justified, regenerated, and initially sanctified. Justification is the forgiveness of his sins and his acceptance with God. ... At the same instant he is born again, renewed, changed from death to life. ... At that same moment there is a deliverance from sinning, a breaking of the power of sin, and a beginning of holiness or perfection. This last can be properly classified as initial sanctification [Leo Cox, *John Wesley's Concept of Perfection*, p. 86]. This is positional holiness.

Participation in the divine nature produces victory over sin. God's seed remains in us enabling us not to sin (1 John 3:9; 1 Peter 1:23). This is Peter's primary emphasis because of the clause which follows—the result of partaking of the divine nature is that we escape the corruption in the world caused by corrupt desires.

When do we escape this corruption? Some theologies say only at death, but the aorist participle in 2 Peter 1:4 puts that escape in the past. According to 2 Peter 2:20, we escape the corruption of this world by knowing our Lord and Savior Jesus Christ. Therefore, the new birth enables us to live a victorious life, in contrast to the defeated life described in Romans 7. 2 Cor 5:17 teaches deliverance from sin. We die to the old life (Romans 6).

In the New Testament every Christian is a "saint" or holy one. The process of being made holy begins upon receiving the Holy Spirit in regeneration. At the new birth we are cleansed from acquired depravity (Titus 3:5; 1 Cor 6:11). While inherited depravity or original sin remains, it no longer controls. It remains, but does not reign. All true Christians are holy, but according to 2 Corinthians 7:1 that holiness may be perfected or completed.

> 1B. *Progressive/continual sanctification* is the gradual and continuous work of the Spirit, beginning with prevenient grace and continuing throughout the Christian life, until final glorification. The Holy Spirit is continually sanctifying us, conforming us to the image of God's Son. In this sense, the work of sanctification is never ending in this life. We are always in the process of being sanctified by the continual application of the blood of Christ to our lives. 1 John 1:7 says it is as we walk in the light as he is in the light that we have fellowship one with another and the blood of Jesus cleanses (present tense = goes on cleansing) us from all sin.

> 1C. *Entire sanctification* is the condition of loving God with the whole heart, mind, soul and strength. The doctrine of entire sanctification is perhaps the most misunderstood doctrine of the Wesleyan movement. We will cover this topic a little more thoroughly than some of the other subjects in this text for two reasons. First, entire sanctification is a distinctive doctrine of the Wesleyan-Arminian movement. That is, the doctrine of entire sanctification is taught more frequently, more fully, and more emphatically by those of Wesleyan-Arminian persuasion than by any other evangelical Christian group. But the second, and perhaps the more important reason at this point in church history, is that the doctrine is misunderstood and misrepresented by those of other theological persuasions, and even by those who purport to believe and teach it.

> 1D. *Final sanctification*, often called glorification, is attained in the resurrection when we are delivered from the very presence of sin. Paul makes this distinction in Philippians 3:12, 15.

✓Interview Question: What do you believe about the nature and work of sanctification?

2. The Experience of Entire Sanctification and the Life of Holiness

The work of the Holy Spirit in entire sanctification has sometimes been misrepresented to include sinless, almost angelic perfection, or such a perfection as can come only when one is glorified. Some represent it to be a kind of Wesleyan eternal security, seeming to believe that once a person has an experience of sanctification, nothing they do from then on is sinful. If you're sanctified, then whatever you are experiencing in your Christian life must be human imperfection and not sin—even if the Scripture is clear that a wrong attitude or a particular habit is sinful.

Sinless, angelic or Adamic perfection is not attainable in this life. Nevertheless, this is not to say that the sanctified Christian makes a practice of known, willful and continuous sinning. In the work of entire sanctification, the Holy Spirit works in the heart of the believer to bring about such complete surrender to God, such freedom from the regular practice of known sin, such freedom from worldliness and the works of the flesh, and in such great measure that it can only be spoken of properly as entire sanctification. Wesley said that entire sanctification often comes to maturer Christians who have been disciples of Jesus for a long while. This is not to say that it *must* be that way, but that often it has been so.

The apostle Paul prays for such entire sanctification when, in 1 Thessalonians 5:23 he says, "And may the very God of peace sanctify you wholly—i.e. completely, or through and through." The word for "wholly" is *holoteleis*, meaning perfect, complete in all respects. He does not claim it as a reality for the Thessalonians at the time of his writing. However, he stands out in front of the Thessalonians in terms of his relationship to God, calling to them to come to where he is. He speaks of whole or entire sanctification as the preferred condition for the believers, and includes the hope that they will be kept blameless at the coming of Christ.

Strictly speaking, entire sanctification is the condition of loving God with all your heart, mind, soul and strength. It is the fulfillment of the first and greatest commandment. This love expels all sin, cleansing the heart from all unrighteousness. Entire sanctification is attainable in earthly life, but it is not the cheap grace many claim by a second trip to the altar. Entire sanctification is the cleansing of the mind, soul and spirit which comes in response to a full consecration of the entire being to God in a complete sacrifice of oneself to the perfect will of God. Because the Holy Spirit of God has control over this person in a way not known before such consecration, he can and does indwell the heart in a manner not known before consecration, resulting in a greater fullness of the Spirit in one's life.

Entire sanctification is not a Wesleyan form of eternal security, whereby those who are entirely sanctified are automatically kept from sin and falling away. On the contrary, the life of sanctification must be maintained even more diligently than the life prior to entire sanctification. Many have experienced periods of life when they knew their lives to be completely surrendered to God, and sanctified with the presence of the Holy Spirit in an unusual way which could only be described as entire; but many of these same people have confessed to periods of time after such experiences when they became aware that their lives were not being lived at such a high level of spiritual reality as before. While they had not been engaged in intentional and continued sin, insofar as they were aware of it, they have experienced the "leaky vessel" syndrome of Hebrews 2.

Wesley argued for entire sanctification on four biblical grounds:

1. Entire sanctification is promised.
2. Prayers were offered for entire sanctification.
3. Christ commanded perfection.
4. The New Testament gives examples of sanctification.

This term (entire sanctification) corresponds with the term *Christian perfection*, but neither term implies the end of growth or progress. *Perfection*, in its absolute sense, is an attribute of God alone (See page 20). Yet Christ commands us to "be perfect" (Matt 5:48). John Fletcher defined Christian perfection as "that maturity of grace and holiness which established adult believers attain under the Christian dispensation" [*Works*, 2:492]. John Wesley explained,

> By "perfection," I mean "perfect love," or the loving God with all our heart, so as to rejoice evermore, to pray without ceasing, and in everything to give thanks. I am convinced every believer may attain this; yet I do not say, he is in a state of damnation, or under the curse of God, till he does attain [*Works*, 12:227].

Christian perfection is a *relative* perfection. The word for perfection most often used in the New Testament is *teleioo* and its related forms. When used in reference to Christian life and experience, this word does not connote the absolute perfection of God, but a maturity or completion, or the reaching of one's intended goal in this life—the goal to love God with all your heart and to love your neighbor as yourself.

A perfect Christian would not have the knowledge of angels. He would not have the innocence Adam and Eve had before the fall [Wesley, "On Perfection," Sermon #76]. Christian perfection should not be confused with a psychological disorder called "perfectionism," which is an attempt to maintain a status of the absence of mistakes or errors. The highest perfection we can attain in this life does not exclude ignorance, error, and a thousand other infirmities. John Wesley stated,

> They [perfected Christians] are not perfect in knowledge. They are not free from ignorance, no, nor from mistake. We are no more to expect any living man to be infallible, than to be omniscient. They are not free from infirmities, such as weakness or slowness of understanding, irregular quickness or heaviness of imagination. Such in another kind are impropriety of language, ungracefulness of pronunciation; to which one might add a thousand nameless defects, either in conversation or behavior [*A Plain Account of Christian Perfection*].

However, 1 John 2:12-14 does imply a maturity in the faith. <u>Little children</u> have the forgiveness of sins. <u>Young men</u> have a strong faith through which they have won some battles and overcome the evil one. <u>Fathers</u> have known God from the beginning point of the new birth and still know him. While the new Christian both fears and loves God, the mature Christian has a perfect love which drives out fear (1 John 4:17-18).

All Christian theological systems teach sanctification, but disagree as to how much progress can be made in this life. Wesleyanism is pessimistic about man's nature, but optimistic about God's grace. The Wesleyan emphasis is the most optimistic position (see Eph 3:20; 1 Thess 5:24). Richard Watson, the first Methodist theologian, was also the first theologian to assign a separate chapter to entire sanctification, treating it as a further benefit of redemption [*Theological Institutes,* 2:450-467].

Yet, we must concede that some people are more spiritual than their theology, and the Holy Spirit works in all true Christians regardless of their theological bias. It should not be assumed that professing agreement with the Wesleyan doctrine automatically produces spiritual superiority.

We believe that full sanctification was provided by the atoning work of Christ as a present possibility (Eph 5:25-26). Other theological systems teach it is possible only after this life.

This deeper relationship is entered and maintained by faith. "Did you receive the Spirit by observing the law, or by believing what you heard? Are you so foolish? After beginning with the Spirit, are you now trying to attain your goal by human effort?" (Gal 3:2-3). Our faith must be in the atoning work of Christ, not in our works.

3. Crisis and Process

We surrender to the Lordship of Christ when we are regenerated. As sinners we are afraid of God's wrath. However, we do not really know at that time what God's will involves. There may be many points in time in which we accept the will of God as it unfolds. The Spirit of God will convict us of inner attitudes which are inconsistent. As a child of God our consecration is based on love.

The same Greek word is used in Romans 6:13 to describe the surrender of a sinner and in Romans 12:1 to describe the consecration of a believer. Each person consecrates to the level of light received. Thus, the consecration of a believer is of a different quality than the surrender of a person coming to Christ for salvation.

Holiness theology often makes a second crisis of our will the end instead of the means to the end. Mildred Wynkoop declared, "There is too much confidence put in the 'crisis experiences' to solve all human problems. The means (the crisis) becomes the end (perfection)" [*A Theology of Love*, p. 47]. The emphasis should not be upon "getting an experience," but upon living a holy life. Kenneth Kinghorn explained

> Growth in the Lord, for most Christians, involves both moments of crises and periods of process. By crises I mean those special times when we consciously make deeper commitments to Christ, as the Holy Spirit reveals personal needs and deeper possibilities. By process I mean the daily growth in grace that we undergo as we walk in faithful obedience to Christ ["Question and Answer," *Asbury Herald*, Summer, 1992, p. 9].

John Wesley emphasized both crisis and process. The process may not be exactly the same for each believer. Thomas Ralston wrote, "It matters but little whether this eminent state of holiness be gained by a bold, energetic, and determined exercise of faith and prayer, or by a more gradual process, whether it be *instantaneous* or *gradual*, or both the one and the other" [*Elements of Divinity*, p. 470].

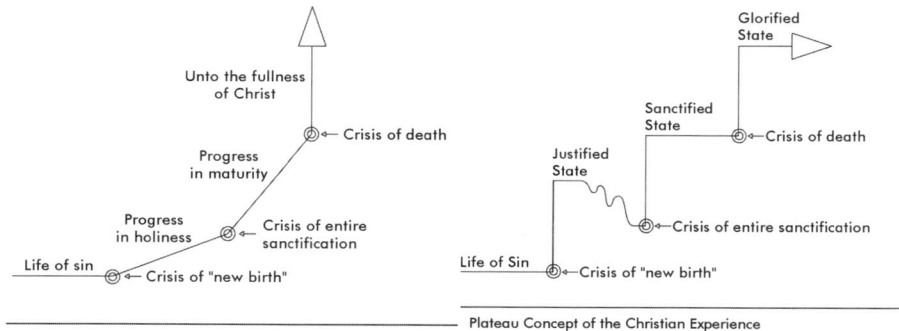

Dynamic Concept of the Christian Experience | Plateau Concept of the Christian Experience

[from *Wesleyan Theological Journal* 4:1 (Spring 1969), p. 14. Used by permission]

4. Entire Sanctification/Perfecting Grace

Can sanctification be entire? We cannot put limits upon the sovereign grace of God. We must state without equivocation that if God be sovereign, there is no limit to the grace he can extend to his creation.

We believe sanctification *can* and *should* be entire in the sense that it reverses the moral depravity of the Fall. To clarify, total depravity came about as a result of original sin. That depravity is extensive in nature, meaning that it adversely affects the entire human personality. Entire sanctification is entire in the sense that it introduces perfecting grace into the entire human personality.

Perfecting grace is not a static condition, but a dynamic relationship with God. The sanctified life is a present tense dynamic, not a once-for-all experience. Therefore, we are cleansed from sin as we walk in the light (1 John 1:9). The love of God in us casts out or expels fear (1 John 4:18). The believer walks with God in an ever deepening relationship of love and holiness. "We teach, therefore not a *state of purity*, but a *maintained condition of purity*, a moment-by-moment salvation consequent upon a moment-by-moment obedience and trust" [Thomas Cook, *New Testament Holiness*, p. 43].

Having clarified that, we also need to note that believers are usually cleansed to their level of consciousness or maturity. We can love God with all our heart, and soul, and mind, and strength and love our neighbor as ourselves. This occurs as we trust Christ moment-by-moment and are moment-by-moment cleansed by his blood and filled with his Spirit. Yet there may be moments when we realize an attitude, a word, or a deed was not Christlike. These may be revelations of deeper needs and become crisis points at which we repent as believers and surrender anew to his Lordship [See Wesley, Sermon #14, *Repentance of Believers*].

5. Ethical and Moral Purity

The Wesleyan emphasis is not upon the Old Testament ceremonial holiness which is so important in high church liturgy. Nor is it the emotional emphasis of pentecostalism. Instead our emphasis is upon an ethical holiness which is exhibited by conformity to the law of God. Anyone who claims holiness or perfection while living a lawless lifestyle is a fanatic.

As we trust Christ each moment, we are cleansed by his blood and filled with his Spirit (Eph 5:18, 1 Jn 1:9). The Holy Spirit develops Christian character and maturity within those who are consistently led by the Spirit (Rom 8:14, Heb 6:1, John 15:2). Those who walk closest to God are the most conscious of their imperfections. The fruit of the Spirit can be increased in quality and quantity. The mature Christian can have a greater delight in God's law and a greater consistency in keeping it. He may enjoy a greater sense of God's favor and a full assurance of faith. He can have a greater sensitivity and compassion for his neighbor. This is Christian perfection.

A genuine movement of God will be characterized by the seeking after more of God's love. For as Wesley cautioned

> If you are seeking anything but more love you are looking wide of the mark, you are getting out of the royal way. When others ask, "Have you received this or that blessing?" if they mean anything but more love, they are leading you out of the way and putting you on a false scent [*A Plain Account of Christian Perfection*].

6. The Gift of Tongues

Is the gift of tongues the evidence of this deeper work of the Spirit?

6A. We are not to seek a particular gift; the Holy Spirit divides them as He wills. After giving a listing of spiritual gifts (*charismata*) in 1 Corinthians 12:11, Paul teaches that the Holy Spirit gives them to each man, just as he determines. If there are as many as twenty-six gifts of the Spirit listed in the Scripture, why insist that only one is the initial evidence of the Holy Spirit?[2]

6B. According to 1 Corinthians 12:30, all do not speak in tongues. Literally it reads, not all speak with tongues. Six times in Acts the Holy Spirit was given; three times the phenomenon of tongues was present and three times it was absent.

6C. According to 1 Corinthians 14:22 tongues is a sign to the unbeliever, not a sign to the believer that he or she has the Holy Spirit. In other words, their purpose is evangelistic, not confirmatory. Therefore, tongues are to be interpreted so that everyone will know what has been said (1 Cor 14:32). And tongues are to be used one at a time, at the most three in any given instance (1 Cor 14:29).

6D. The genuine gift of tongues is real languages. In Acts 2:8-11, 15 regions or dialects are mentioned. Everyone heard in their own language. In both Acts and 1 Corinthians, the word "unknown" is italicized and not in the original text. Glossolalia means known languages. Some have concluded that Paul references speaking the language of angels, not men in 1 Corinthians 13:1. However, this sentence structure is what is known as a third class condition, "even if I could speak with the tongues of . . . angels." With this structure, Paul appears to be overstating his argument with an exaggeration to make a point. Nowhere else in Scripture is an angelic language mentioned and this verse does not establish that men do/can speak in angelic languages.

6E. Tongues can be easily counterfeited. A physical phenomenon therefore does not evidence a spiritual reality. Today people are coached. They are to abandon control and just say anything. But according to 1 Corinthians 14:32 "the spirit of the prophets are subject to the control of the prophets." The indwelling of the Spirit gives us greater

---

[2] At least four major passages in the New Testament deal with the subject of the gifts of the Spirit. Romans 12:3-8, 1 Cor 12:1-31, Ephesians 4:11-16, 1 Peter 4:10. Some people add gifts from the Old Testament, such as Bezaleel's gift of craftsmanship, and so on. There are a number of different categorizations of the gifts, each of which is helpful. The important issue is not that there are differences of opinions on the gifts of the Spirit, but that the Spirit gives gifts to every believer to use for the profit of all. And Paul says we should desire spiritual gifts, especially the best gifts, but we should be more interested that we might proclaim the truth of God so that everyone could understand it (1 Cor 14:1).

self-control, not the loss of self control. It is a dangerous practice to open yourself to anything and become passive. God does not bypass our minds, but enlightens our mind.

6F. Tongues-speaking does not produce holy living. Stanley Horton, Assembly of God scholar, admitted the following, "The baptism in the Holy Spirit (i.e. speaking in tongues) is not of itself a sanctifying experience" [*Five Views on Sanctification*, p. 132].

7. What God's Sanctifying Grace Can Do for You

7A. God's sanctifying grace can realign attitudes, heal damaged emotions, make us whole.

7B. God's sanctifying grace can strengthen, empower, establish our faith; a full assurance of faith.

7C. God's sanctifying grace can enlarge our capacity to receive a greater measure of the Spirit.

7D. God's sanctifying grace can increase our love and all the fruit of the Spirit. "Every branch in me that bears fruit, he purges it that it may bring forth more fruit" (John 15:2). The fruit of the Spirit can increase in quality and quantity.

7E. God's sanctifying grace can enable us to acquire maturity in knowledge, spiritual insight, discernment.

7F. God's sanctifying grace can give us a greater delight in God's law and a greater consistency in keeping it.

7G.. God's sanctifying grace can provide us with a greater sensitivity toward spiritual realities and a greater compassion for his neighbor. More sensitivity toward our neighbor and a purer ethic in our relationships; a maturity of character.

7H. God's sanctifying grace can unite our will. "To be pure in heart is to will one thing" (Kierkegaard). This is a perfection of motive.

7I. God's sanctifying grace can reveal a greater knowledge of God and of the substance of God's will.

7J. God's sanctifying grace can give us a greater comprehension of the Lordship of Christ.

7K. God's sanctifying grace can lead us to a deeper surrender based upon a deeper revelation.

7L. God's sanctifying grace can bring about death to selfishness—not self; death to carnal traits, not to personality.

7M. God's sanctifying grace can confirm the heart with a greater sense of God's favor and assurance that we are pleasing God.

7N. God's sanctifying grace can empower with the characteristics described in 1 Cor 13:4-7 displacing all sin.

7O. God's sanctifying grace can result in a pure heart, cleansed from all unrighteousness (1 John 1:9).

7P. God's sanctifying grace can give us the mind of Christ; Christlikeness.

7Q. God's sanctifying grace can give us a holy optimism that enables us to be positive while persevering.

Every true Christian hungers for these dynamics. "Make me as holy as a saved sinner can be," prayed Robert Murray M'Cheyne. Even though Calvinistic theology offers no hope of deliverance from sin in this life, there is still a desire to rise above it.

This sanctifying work of the Spirit occurs in all true believers, whether or not they embrace Wesleyan theology. While it is not necessary to adhere to a particular theological system to experience the grace, it is the duty of the Church to counsel, teach, and provide spiritual guidance for believers. The Wesleyan synthesis is the most adequate framework in which to diagnose spiritual needs, discern spiritual imbalance, and direct spiritual formation.

✓Interview Question: What do you believe about holiness of heart and life?

For Further Reading:

Cox, Leo. *John Wesley's Concept of Perfection*. Kansas City: Beacon Hill, 1964.

Hunt, John. *Letters on Sanctification*. 1849. Rpt. Salem, OH: Schmul Publishers, 1984.

Parsons, Elmer E. *Living the Holy Life Today*. Indianapolis: Light and Life, 1990.

Wesley, John. *A Plain Account of Christian Perfection* in Volume 11 of *Works* and in various booklet forms. "On Perfection," Sermon #76.

Wynkoop, Mildred. *A Theology of Love*. Kansas City: Beacon Hill, 1972.

Chapter Eleven

The Doctrine of the Church

The Church is the community of the redeemed; it is a colony of heaven. The Church is composed of those who have responded to God's call and are saved through Christ. They are under the leadership of the Spirit and are the instrument of God through which he carries out his purposes in the world.

1. The Origin of the Church

God has always had a people. We see the beginnings of the church within the first family. Adam was the first priest and he led his family in worship through sacrifices. As the world became apostate, God called Noah out. The basic meaning of the Greek word for church, *ekklesia*, means called out. The ark is an illustration of the Church. We are called out of this world to be saved from coming judgment.

Abraham was called out and entered into a covenant agreement with God. By the time of Moses, the family had grown into a nation. The nation of Israel was God's Church in the Old Testament. Acts 7:38 refers to the Israelites as the "church in the wilderness." By the New Testament, the Church was no longer national, but international. The mystery referred to by Paul was that God intended both Jew and Gentile to be one body (Eph 3:4-6). Abraham is the father of all who believe (Rom 4:12, 16). We are chosen by grace, not race (Rom 2:28-29). We are the new Israel (Gal 6:16).

2. The Marks of the Church

The Methodist Articles of Religion state, "The visible Church of Christ is a congregation of faithful men, in which the pure Word of God is preached, and the sacraments duly administered, according to Christ's ordinance" [McClintock and Strong, *Cyclopedia of Biblical, Theological and Ecclesiastical Literature*, 1867-1887; Rpt. Baker, 1:443]. Classic Protestantism usually added the mark of the exercise of discipleship, or accountability, for the Christian life [Oden, *Systematic Theology*, 3:299-301].

We believe there is a fourth mark of the church—divine love. Jesus said, "By this shall all men know that ye are my disciples, if ye have love one to another" (John 13:35). Francis Schaeffer called Christian love the "final apologetic." [*Works*, 4:188-204. See also pp. 151-52 for applying this mark to the church].

These same marks actually have been part of the Church since the time of the Apostles. [See also Carter, Charles W, ed. *A Contemporary Wesleyan Theology*, Zondervan, 1983, 2:585-590].

3. The Essential Characteristics of the Church

3A. Universal, yet local

The word "catholic" means universal. We affirm that the Church is catholic. We do not confuse the true catholicity of the church with the earthly organization called the Roman Catholic Church. The term "Roman Catholic" refers to the organization centered in Rome. The headquarters for the true catholic Church is in heaven. While Rome still claims that the whole of the Christian church is under its jurisdiction by right of Apostolic Succession and the authority of the pope, we deny any organic or organizational connection to the Roman See.

The Old Testament Church was limited to a small part of Palestine. Many of the laws and ceremonies were only adaptable locally. However God intended Israel to bless the world. The prophets foretold worldwide influence.

When Jesus came, however, he found God's people to be proud and uninterested in outreach. Christ made it clear the new Church was to be universal in passages such as: Matt 28:19, Luke 2:10, John 4:20-21.

The Church is universal because:

1. All believers are under the same Lord.
2. The Church's mission is a world vision.
3. The sacraments are universally adaptable.
4. God has determined that the Church will be made up of all nations (Rev 7:9).

Often when "church" is used in the singular and is not qualified by a location, it is referring to the universal Church. For example, Matthew 16:18 does not promise that a local assembly cannot fail, but that the universal Church will never fail. "The one, holy, universal church is promised imperishable continuance, even if particular churches or local bodies or denominations may fail or atrophy" [Oden, *Systematic Theology*, 3:345].

The most common usage in the New Testament for the word "church," however, is in references to local congregations. *Ekklesia* is used 115 times in the New Testament; most references are to local congregations.

New Testament congregations cooperated in these areas:

1. They shared a common faith.
2. They shared a common Scripture.
3. They sent letters of commendation to each other.
4. They cooperated in discipline.
5. They helped each other financially.
6. The cooperated in missions by financially supporting Paul.

3B. United, yet diverse

"There is one body" (Eph 4:6). Jesus prayed that "they all may be one" (John 17:21). God does not want division (Rom 16:17; 1 Cor 1:10). There are 33,820 denominations and paradenominations worldwide [David B. Barrett, ed, *World Christian Encyclopedia*, 2nd ed, Oxford University Press, 2001, 1:10]. The result is overlapping ministries, a competitive spirit, and confusion. What are we to do? John Wesley taught that the unity of the Church is based upon the Christian *koinonia* (fellowship) in the Holy Spirit.

The Roman church has unity, but no liberty. Protestants have liberty, but no unity. They justified the divisions by teaching an invisible unity. The ecumenical movement is willing to sacrifice truth in order to have visible unity. Others denounce all denominations and begin a new one. The best approach is to recognize the unity of God's people and demonstrate a spirit of cooperation. Unity cannot be legislated or organized. It is a reality to be recognized. If God can take 263 bones, 600 muscles, 970 miles of blood vessels, and 10 million nerves and make a body that can function efficiently, his plan is for the body of Christ to work together for his glory.

In order for there to be unity, there need not be uniformity. Cultural difference will exist in a worldwide Church. Local congregations may have different personalities, gifts, and ministries, yet they can complement, not compete with each other.

Sectarianism is sin. Romans 16:17-18 mentions divisions (standing apart). *Hairesis* is translated "factions, divisive, differences, sect" by the NIV and "heresies" in the KJV (Acts 24:14; 1 Cor 11:19; Gal 5:20; Titus 3:10).

John Wesley's sermon on "Catholic Spirit" mentioned modes of worship, forms of government, modes of baptism, types of praying, candidates for baptism, and observation of the Lord's Supper as areas where he had definite convictions, but where he realized all did not agree. He concluded, "Is thine heart right, as my heart is with thy heart? If it be, give me thine hand." [Wesley, *Catholic Spirit*, Sermon #39].

> In essentials - unity
> In nonessentials - liberty
> In all things - charity

This trilogy has been attributed to several people over the centuries, but it is an accurate assessment of the focus of the catholic spirit.

3C. Holy, yet imperfect

The Roman Catholic church and the Eastern Orthodox church both teach there is no salvation outside the Church, which they interpret to be their organization. Therefore everyone must join them to obtain salvation. Other mainline denominations tend to teach that salvation comes sacramentally and, therefore, salvation comes through the Church.

There are other denominations which do not believe there is salvation outside their name or rituals. Often faith is reduced to the affirmation of a creed.

Calvinism believes that the elect are known only to God. Modern evangelicalism does not believe that there are necessarily any distinguishing marks of the saved. They would teach that the invisible Church was pure, but the visible Church was a mixture.

As Wesleyans, we believe that God's Church should be holy, but we have difficulty in measuring spiritual life in those who present themselves for membership.

The Scriptures teach that those who are saved have been added to the Church (Acts 2:47). Therefore the Church is a spiritual organism, not a mixture of saved and unsaved. The holiness of the Church is grounded in the discipline of grace which guides and matures the Christian life from beginning until end. Wesley said that "no unholy man can possibly be a member" of the Church [*Journal* 4:436].

The Reformers taught that the true Church existed where the Word of God was faithfully taught, the sacraments faithfully administered, and discipline or accountability enforced. Martin Luther said the surest mark of the true Church is that in it one hears the pure gospel proclaimed. No secular organization has the authority to administer the sacraments. John Calvin concluded, "Where there is a good faith effort to maintain purity of preaching, lawful sacramental life, and discipline in earnest, one may conscientiously embrace a church even if blemished" [Oden, 3:302, cites Calvin *Institutes* 4.1.12].

We affirm that the Church is a spiritual organization, yet we also observe that local congregations within Scripture had problems (especially at Corinth and five of the seven churches in Revelation 2-3). Perhaps rather than distinguishing between the visible and invisible Church, we should make the distinction between the universal and local Church. Some may be affiliated with a local congregation who are not in God's Church. Jesus made this kind of distinction in the parable of the tares (Matt 13:29-30).

3D. Apostolic, yet contemporary

According to 1 Corinthians 3:10-11 Jesus Christ is the Church's one foundation. However, in Ephesians 2:20 the apostles were given the authority to lay the foundation which was based on their instruction from Jesus Christ. The Church is to teach the apostles' doctrine. A church is apostolic when it preaches the apostles' doctrine (Acts 2:42). Christ empowered the apostles. They left no successors. Their authority remains in their letters which comprise the New Testament. These letters give the qualifications for the selection of leadership (1 Tim 3; Titus 1). The Church is apostolic to the degree that it is faithful to the apostolic witness. There has been an uninterrupted apostolic witness to the gospel through a faithful community and faithful ministers down through history. The Church is God's appointed means of upholding truth (1 Tim 3:15).

While doctrine, experience, and the mission of the Church do not change, methodology and forms can and do change to meet the various and changing needs of the society to which the church ministers.

✓ Interview Question: What do you understand to be the nature of the church and its relationship to Christ?

4. The Ministry of the Church; the Gifts of the Spirit

The gifts are listed in Romans 12:6-8; 1 Cor 12:7-11, 28-31; Eph 4:11. They correspond to the mission of the Church. Every believer has a gift (1 Cor 12:7; 1 Peter 4:10) and each gift is given for the building up of the body of Christ:

Communication Gifts (the mouth)

prophecy
teaching
evangelism
languages (for more discussion of this gift, see pp. 65-67).
interpretation

Counseling Gifts (the heart)

exhortation
word of knowledge
word of wisdom
discernment of spirits

Confirmation Gifts (the eye)

faith
gifts of healing
miracles

Coordination Gifts (the brain)

leadership
administration
pastor

Caring Gifts (the hand)

giving
helps
hospitality
mercy
service

Commission Gifts (the feet)

missionary

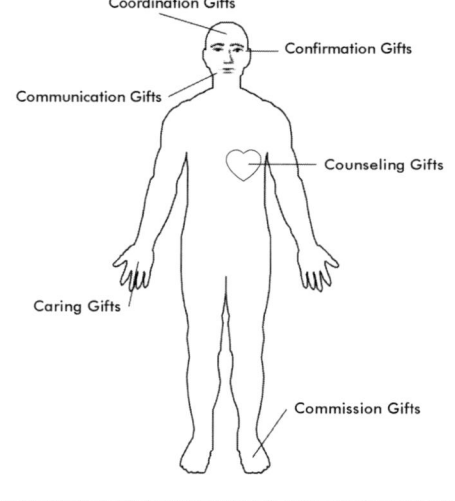

The Body of Christ

5. The Sacraments of the Church

A *sacrament* is an outward and visible sign of an inward and spiritual grace given unto us; having been instituted and ordained by Christ himself, as a means by which we receive grace. This grace is not automatically imparted through the ritual; it is imparted by a faith in Christ which leads us to obey his command. The sacraments are God's pledge or seal to assure us that we have been forgiven, received the Spirit, and adopted into the family of God. We receive strength and confirmation through the sacraments.

1. A sacrament must be instituted by divine authority. Christ, the head of the Church, observed and instituted both baptism and communion. Furthermore, both are commanded by Christ. Water baptism is commanded (Matt 28:19). The Lord's Supper is commanded (1 Cor 11:24,26). 1 Corinthians 11:2 calls the Lord's Supper an "ordinance" which has been passed down from Christ.

2. A sacrament must possess a symbolic character. It is an outward sign of an inward grace.

3. A sacrament is a seal of the covenant. The Roman army soldiers were required to pledge obedience to the commander and this act was called a "sacrament." The Lord's Supper is a pledge of our faith.

4. The sacraments are means of grace. The means of grace are spiritual disciplines which people use to express their faith and receive God's grace.

Wesley Stated, "By 'means of grace' I understand outward signs, words, or actions, ordained of God, and appointed for this end, to be the ordinary channels whereby he might convey to men, preventing, justifying, or sanctifying grace" ["The Means of Grace," sermon #16].

Wesley designated the instituted means of grace as: prayer, searching the Scriptures, the Lord's Supper, fasting, Christian conference or fellowship. These are ongoing sacraments, but note that baptism, although a sacrament, is not listed here because it is not repeated.

As a Fellowship we generally recognize two sacraments – baptism and the Lord's Supper or Communion. We take a position between sacramentalism and a view of the sacraments as superficial ordinances. This means that we believe God actually communicates grace to those receiving the sacrament, as they look forward to Christ in faith.[3]

Sacramentalism exalts the sacraments to the point that faith for salvation is placed in the proper observance of ritual. [Reasoner and Brush, eds, *The*

Wesley Workbook, Fundamental Wesleyan Publishers, 1996, p. 93]. On the other hand, some take such a low view of both baptism and the Lord's Supper that they are almost ritualistic nuisances, rather than obedience to the will of God and enjoyment of the real presence of God.

As a Fellowship, we take a mediating position which incorporates both presence and obedient faith. Thus, with regard to the Lord's supper, we agree with Harper's statement, "By his own choice the risen Christ is truly present whenever the Lord's Supper is observed. Christ does not come through the bread and cup; he comes through the Spirit. But Christ is *really* there" [Steve Harper, *Devotional Life in the Wesleyan Tradition*, p. 38].

We also believe that the sacrament of water baptism is the outward testimony of the inward work of the Holy Spirit in regeneration. Baptism itself does not save; nor is baptism required before one can be saved. However, water baptism follows the example set for us by our Lord in the fulfillment of righteousness, and it is a means by which confirming grace is communicated to the believer. In *A Treatise on Baptism,* John Wesley defined this rite as "the initiatory sacrament, which enters us into covenant with God. It was instituted by Christ, who alone has power to institute a proper sacrament, a sign, seal, pledge, and means of grace, perpetually obligatory on all Christians" [*Works*, 10:188].

As a Fellowship, we are in line with the historic Wesleyan-Arminian tradition with regard to the subjects of the mode of baptism and the baptism of infants, leaving such questions to the discretion of biblically informed and godly conscience.

6. The Mission of the Church

There have been many attempts to define the mission of the church. Almost all of these attempts hold that the church has three basic mission responsibilities—to love and glorify God, to love our neighbor as ourselves,

---

[3] Some see Christ's work of foot washing in the upper room as the institution of a third sacrament. While the Fellowship does not deny the spiritual and emotional undertones of such a ceremony, and while we do not condemn the use of the ceremony, we see Christ's work of foot washing as a teaching tool by which he stressed the necessity of Christian servanthood, not as a sacrament by which he communicates grace to the believer.

and to participate in the completion of the Great Commission. These are considered below under three distinct titles.

> 6A. Our responsibility toward God—Worship. The Father seeks true worship" (John 4:23). The Westminster Catechism of the 17th century asked, What is the chief end of man? The answer given was, To glorify God and to enjoy him forever.

The issue in worship is not traditional or contemporary, but worship which glorifies God and sanctifies man. Good worship is sanctifying. Misguided worship—entertainment, psychological or cultural worship cannot sanctify because it does not glorify God. It is man-centered rather than God-centered. Worship should include the entire human personality—mind, will and emotions.

A. W. Tozer wrote, "Worship is to feel in your heart and express in some appropriate manner a humbling but delightful sense of admiring awe and astonished wonder and overpowering love in the presence of the most ancient Mystery, that Mystery which philosophers call the First Cause but which we call Our Father Which Art in Heaven" [*Keys to the Deeper Life*, Zondervan, 1957, p. 80].

> 6B. Our responsibility to each other - discipleship: teaching, edification, fellowship, counsel. We are dependant upon the body of Christ to receive these ministries. "No one can develop a mature spirituality alone. To be a Christian is to be called into community. It is to become a functioning part of the body of Christ" [Steve Harper, *Devotional Life in the Wesleyan Tradition*, p. 54].

The "one another (*allalon*)" passages in the New Testament exhort us to "make every effort to do what leads to peace and to mutual edification (Rom 14:19).

"Build yourselves up in your most holy faith" (Jude 20).

"Grow and build itself (the whole body) up in love as each part does it work" (Eph 4:16).

"Admonish one another" (Rom 15:14).

"Consider how we may spur one another on toward love and good deeds. Let us not give up meeting together . . . but let us encourage one another" (Heb 10:24-25).

Comfort one another (1 Thess 4:18; 5:11)

Encourage one another (Heb 3:13)

Confess to one another (James 5:16)

Pray for one another and carry each other's burdens (Gal 6:2)

Live in harmony with one another; be sympathetic, love as brothers, be compassionate and humble (1 Peter 3:8). This love for each other is a prerequuisite for evangelism. "By this all men will know that you are my disciples, if you love one another" (John 13:35).

    6C. Our responsibility to the world - missions, evangelism, social action.

Jesus said, "Go into all the world and make disciples of all peoples." In so doing, he put missions and evangelism on the front burner of the New Testament Church's activity.

The word "missionary" means "sent out." It is the Latin equivalent to the Greek word "apostle." It describes someone who crosses cultural or geographic barriers to carry out the great commission.

Evangelism means to preach or proclaim the Gospel. We are to give an answer to everyone who asks the reason for the hope we have (1 Peter 3:15).

Jesus also taught us to pray, "Thy will be done on earth as it is in heaven." Part of the Gospel is the call to repentance. As our brother's keeper, the Church must stand against sin and call the world to turn from sin (Gen 4:9). Thus we are called to take a stand against social ills and to work for the establishment of the Kingdom of Christ on earth.

✓ Interview Question: What do you believe about the mission of the church? What is your commitment to the Great Commission? What social issues do you believe your congregation needs to address in order to minister to its community?

For Further Reading:

Harper, Steve. *Devotional Life in the Wesleyan Tradition*. Nashville: Upper Room, 1983.

Wesley, John. "The Means of Grace," Sermon #16.

Chapter Twelve

The Doctrine of Last Things

The Greek word for "last things" is *eschatos*. "Eschatology" refers to the biblical teachings concerning events which will occur at the end of world history. The "last days" is the period between Christ's first advent and second advent (Heb 1:1-2). There will be a "last day" when Christ returns.

We must be cautious about making dogmatic assertions concerning the future. Some professional scholars in Jesus' day expected two Messiahs, one to suffer and one to reign. They expected the establishment of a political kingdom which would overthrow Rome. Christ fulfilled 332 distinct prophecies, yet he was rejected because he did not fit their scheme. If the experts missed it concerning his first advent, we should guard against prophetic speculation.

Approximately 20-25% of the Bible was prophetic when written. Prophecy serves to

1. Authenticate the Scripture. However, when prophecy "experts" make outlandish claims which do not come to pass, the Bible is discredited.

2. Give hope to the Christian that God is in control. History is linear, not circular. Human existence has meaning as we move toward God's ultimate purpose.

3. Warn the sinner of coming judgment.

Five Prophetic Fundamentals

1. The literal return of Jesus Christ; the second advent. It is claimed that the second coming of Christ is mentioned over 300 times in the New Testament. Not every "coming" of Christ, however, is the second advent.

   1A. Christ came through the Incarnation (1 John 4:2-3).

1B. Christ came to the disciples after his resurrection (John 16:16).

1C. Christ came on the day of Pentecost (Matt 16:28; John 14:18).

1D. Christ comes for the Christian at death.

1E. Christ comes often in judgment (Rev 2:5, 16).

1F. Christ comes often in revival (Acts 3:20).

1G. Christ comes to the believer in salvation (Rev 3:20).

1H. Christ comes when believers assemble (Matt 18:20).

2. The resurrection of all mankind from the dead.

The soul is immortal, but the body will be resurrected. John said that at the coming of Christ death will give up the dead (Rev 20:13). This describes a general resurrection when the sea and death and hades (the grave) surrendered every person back to life. This description alone destroys the teaching of conditional immortality and annihilation.

Supporting Scriptures: Dan 12:2, John 5:28-29, 1 Cor 15:42-44, Rev 20:12-13.

3. The final judgment

    3A. The judgment will follow Christ's return: Acts 17:31, 1 Cor 4:5, Rev 22:12.

    3B. All will be judged: Rom 14:10-12, 2 Cor 5:10, Rev 20:12-13.

    3C. The basis of judgment will be two-fold, whether our name is written in the Lamb's Book of Life, and according to our works (Rev 20:11-15). We are saved by faith, but we demonstrate true faith by good works (James 2:17-26).

4. Heaven

Heaven is a real place (John 14:2-3). It is a place of rest, but not inactivity (Rev 7:15; 22:3). It will be deliverance from temptation, Satan, infirmities, pain, and death (Rev 21-22). We are told 51 times that heaven is forever. Heaven will be a holy place. It will be full of praise and music. It will be a place of reunion with loved ones who have died in the faith. Most importantly we will see God (1 John 3:2).

5. Hell

The Bible has more to say about hell than about heaven. If you accept the authority of Scripture you cannot deny the existence of hell.

The Hebrew *sheol* and the Greek *hades* usually refer to the grave, but sometimes they specifically mean a place of torment. The Greek words *gehenna* and *tartarus* are also translated "hell." *Gehenna* is used twelve times and *tartarus* is used once in the New Testament. These words are always used to describe a place of torment.

It is often asked how a loving God can send people to hell. God is not only a God of love, but of holiness (Hab 1:13), justice (Rev 15:3), and mercy (Micah 7:18). Those who go to hell have rejected God's mercy and his offer of salvation.

Hell is eternal. Revelation 20:10 says those in the lake of fire will be tormented day and night for ever and ever. This phrase "for ever and ever" is the strongest term in Greek. It is also used to refer to the duration of God's own existence in Revelation 1:18; 4:9-10; 10:6; 15:7. According to Matthew 25:46 the duration of heaven is the same length as the duration of hell because the same adjective *aionion* is used to describe both.

Hell is described symbolically in Revelation as:

5A. the lake of fire and brimstone (or sulfur)

5B. the second death - symbolizes eternal separation from God. Just as there is a new and higher life in the Spirit, so there is also a second and deeper death.

To say these expressions are symbolic in no way tones down the awfulness of eternal punishment. Martin Luther said that no picture of hell could be as bad as the reality. Sometimes preaching has centered on the physical suffering and pain, but John uses words such as fire and death to describe something which is even worse.

"Fleeing the wrath to come" was a major theme in the preaching of early Methodism. John Wesley wrote to William Law

> Now this much cannot be denied, that these texts speak as if there were really such a place as hell ... I would then ask but one plain question: If the case is not so, why did God speak as if it was? Say you, "To affright men from sin"? What, by guile, by dissimulation, by hanging out false colors? Can you conceive the Most High dressing up a scarecrow, as we do to fright children? Far be it from Him! If

there be any such fraud in the Bible, the Bible is not of God. And indeed this must be the result of all ... So that if we give up the one, we must give up the other. No hell, no heaven, no revelation! [*Letters*, 6 Jan. 1756].

Having discussed these five non-negotiable doctrines of eschatology, we recognize that there are differences of interpretation regarding secondary issues such as the nature of the millennium, the timing of the Great Tribulation, the identity of Antichrist, the nature of the Battle of Armageddon, whether a Rapture constitutes a separate second coming of Christ. As a Fellowship, we have taken a traditional Wesleyan-Arminian position in allowing these differences of interpretation without requiring adherence to any particular speculative position. We have agreed as a body not to create dissension or division over questions which are not clearly grounded in trustworthy biblical exegesis, and/or which historically have not been widely adopted by the general church.

Fellowship History

The International Fellowship of Bible Churches sees itself as part of the people of God. We identify ourselves with the Christian Church which began at Pentecost. Through a common faith we are united with the saints and martyrs of all ages.

We embrace the Apostles, Nicene and Athanasian Creeds as accurate summaries of Biblical truth. These creeds are commonly held by the Church Universal. They were developed by the early church to defend the faith against false teaching. While we respect the convictions of those who are non-creedal, the Latin word *credo* simply means "I believe." We really have no choice of whether we have a "creed" if it is understood in this sense. In reality, our only options are whether our statements of belief are either adequate or inadequate. Taken together, these creeds present adequate statements of belief as developed by saints and martyrs of the early church under the guidance of the Holy Spirit.

The Apostles Creed

I believe in God the Father Almighty, Maker of heaven and earth;

And in Jesus Christ his only Son our Lord; who was conceived by the Holy Ghost, born of the Virgin Mary; suffered under Pontius Pilate; was crucified, dead, and buried; He descended into hell; the third day He rose again from the dead; He ascended into heaven, and sitteth on the right hand of God the Father Almighty; from thence He shall come to judge the quick and the dead.

I believe in the Holy Ghost; the Holy Catholic Church; the communion of saints; the forgiveness of sins; the resurrection of the body; and the life everlasting. Amen.

The Nicene Creed

I believe in one God, the Father Almighty, Maker of heaven and earth, and of all things visible and invisible.

And in one Lord Jesus Christ, the only-begotten Son of God; begotten of His Father before all worlds, God of God, Light of light, Very God of very God, begotten, not made; being of one substance with the Father; by whom all things were made; who for us men and for our salvation came down from heaven, and was incarnate by the Holy Ghost of the Virgin Mary, and was made man; and was crucified also for us under Pontius Pilate; He suffered and was buried; and the third day He arose again according to the Scriptures; and ascended into heaven; and sitteth on the right hand of the Father; and He shall come again, with glory, to judge both the quick and the dead: whose kingdom shall have no end.

And I believe in the Holy Ghost, the Lord and Giver of Life, who proceedeth from the Father and the Son; who with the Father and Son together is worshiped and glorified; who spake by the prophets; and I believe in one Catholic and Apostolic Church; I acknowledge one baptism for the remission of sins; and I look for the resurrection of the dead; and the life of the world to come. Amen.

Athanasian Creed

1. Whosoever will be saved, before all things it is necessary that he hold the catholic faith;
2. Which faith except every one do keep whole and undefiled, without doubt he shall perish everlastingly.
3. And the catholic faith is this: That we worship one God in Trinity, and Trinity in Unity;
4. Neither confounding the persons nor dividing the substance.
5. For there is one person of the Father, another of the Son, and another of the Holy Spirit.
6. But the Godhead of the Father, of the Son, and of the Holy Spirit is all one, the glory equal, the majesty coeternal.
7. Such as the Father is, such is the Son, and such is the Holy Spirit.
8. The Father uncreated, the Son uncreated, and the Holy Spirit uncreated.

9. The Father incomprehensible, the Son incomprehensible, and the Holy Spirit incomprehensible.
10. The Father eternal, the Son eternal, and the Holy Spirit eternal.
11. And yet they are not three eternals but one eternal.
12. As also there are not three uncreated nor three incomprehensible, but one uncreated and one incomprehensible.
13. So likewise the Father is almighty, the Son almighty, and the Holy Spirit almighty.
14. And yet they are not three almighties, but one almighty.
15. So the Father is God, the Son is God, and the Holy Spirit is God;
16. And yet they are not three Gods, but one God.
17. So likewise the Father is Lord, the Son Lord, and the Holy Spirit Lord;
18. And yet they are not three Lords but one Lord.
19. For like as we are compelled by the Christian verity to acknowledge every Person by himself to be God and Lord;
20. So are we forbidden by the catholic religion to say; There are three Gods or three Lords.
21. The Father is made of none, neither created nor begotten.
22. The Son is of the Father alone; not made nor created, but begotten.
23. The Holy Spirit is of the Father and of the Son; neither made, nor created, nor begotten, but proceeding.
24. So there is one Father, not three Fathers; one Son, not three Sons; one Holy Spirit, not three Holy Spirits.
25. And in this Trinity none is afore or after another; none is greater or less than another.
26. But the whole three persons are coeternal, and coequal.
27. So that in all things, as aforesaid, the Unity in Trinity and the Trinity in Unity is to be worshiped.
28. He therefore that will be saved must thus think of the Trinity.
29. Furthermore it is necessary to everlasting salvation that he also believe rightly the incarnation of our Lord Jesus Christ.
30. For the right faith is that we believe and confess that our Lord Jesus Christ, the Son of God, is God and man.
31. God of the substance of the Father, begotten before the worlds; and man of substance of His mother, born in the world.
32. Perfect God and perfect man, of a reasonable soul and human flesh subsisting.
33. Equal to the Father as touching His Godhead, and inferior to the Father as touching His manhood.
34. Who, although He is God and man, yet He is not two, but one Christ.

35. One, not by conversion of the Godhead into flesh, but by taking of that manhood into God.
36. One altogether, not by confusion of substance, but by unity of person.
37. For as the reasonable soul and flesh is one man, so God and man is one Christ;
38. Who suffered for our salvation, descended into hell, rose again the third day from the dead;
39. He ascended into heaven, He sits on the right hand of the Father, God, Almighty;
40. From thence He shall come to judge the quick and the dead.
41. At whose coming all men shall rise again with their bodies;
42. and shall give account of their own works.
43. And they that have done good shall go into life everlasting and they that have done evil into everlasting fire.
44. This is the catholic faith, which except a man believe faithfully he cannot be saved.

✓ Interview Question: What is your conviction about the major tenets of the Christian faith as reflected in the Creeds?

We accept the decisions of the early church councils at Nicea, Constantinople, Ephesus, and Chalcedon which defended the biblical teaching regarding the nature of Christ. These early church councils did not meet to determine doctrine, but to defend the doctrine which had already been once and for all delivered to the church. The church has always had to defend orthodoxy against legalism, mysticism, rationalism, and liberalism.

Across the first centuries of the Christian church a hierarchy developed which violated the simplicity of the New Testament organization. By A. D. 590 Gregory claimed supremacy over the other bishops of the church and functioned as the first pope, thus, in effect, creating the hierarchy of the Roman Catholic Church. In A.D. 1054 the great division between east and west occurred. While there have been great saints and scholars among both the Roman Catholic and Eastern Orthodox Churches, in general they became corrupt and immoral, setting themselves in authority over God's Word.

A thousand years of darkness followed and the message of the gospel was nearly eclipsed. Yet God always had a people. We honor the memory of Savanarola, John Wycliffe and the Lollards, and John Hus, as well as many other nonconformists. The torch of truth kept burning through this period of darkness. In the providence of God, Martin Luther was raised up to lead a reformation. We express our solidarity with the Reformation doctrines of *sola Scriptura, sola fides,* and *sola gratia.* As John Wesley would later declare, the church stands or falls on the doctrine of justification by faith. Since the Roman Catholic Church has never retracted the curse invoked at the Council of Trent which declared anyone who preaches justification by faith alone is under eternal damnation, we remain unapologetic Protestants.

Although we appreciate the contributions of Reformers such as John Calvin and the Anabaptist movement, we believe the greatest reformer was Jacobus Arminius (AD 1560 - 1609). Arminius was able to establish a balance between the humanism of Pelagius and the fatalism of Calvin. We align ourselves with the Arminian interpretation of Scripture which declares:

1. The decree of salvation applies to all who believe on Christ and who persevere in faith and obedience.
2. Christ died for all men.
3. The Holy Spirit must enable us through prevenient grace to repent and believe.
4. God's saving grace is not irresistible.
5. It is possible for those who are truly regenerate to fall from grace if they do not persevere.

The Arminian position was revived by the early Methodists. Methodism was simply a revival of apostolic Christianity. We identify ourselves as Wesleyan-Arminian in doctrine. With Wesley, we hold to the following:

1. The full inspiration, inerrancy, and authority of Scripture.
2. The Fall and sinfulness of mankind.
3. The universal atonement of Christ.
4. Prevenient grace which enables us to obey the commands of the gospel.
5. Justification by faith alone.
6. Regeneration which produces victory over sin through the indwelling Spirit of God.
7. Direct assurance of the Spirit to and with our spirits that we are accepted by God.
8. Christian perfection; a maturity in Christ and a conformity to the character of Christ.
9. The expansion and triumph of God's kingdom through the preaching of the gospel and revival.

Organizational Beginnings

Methodism spread to America, where it became the largest Protestant denomination. By the late Nineteenth Century, Methodism became susceptible to the influences of liberal theology. As a result, many small groups of churches of Methodist background pulled away from the Methodist Church, and the holiness movement became more organized as an entity apart from Methodism. In time, the holiness movement, while claiming Wesley's legacy, moved away from his emphasis on apostolic Christianity. Among many, the holy life was reduced to an experience to be professed, rather than a relationship to be pursued. As a result, the holiness movement became susceptible to legalism and schism, resulting in many small denominations of Methodist descent.

In 1988, a group of leaders came together to promote a new emphasis on grace without lawlessness and to seek God for a revival of apostolic Christianity. A steering committee had spent more than a year in deliberations before the first Assembly of the International Fellowship of Bible Churches, Inc. occurred in August of 1988 at a Baptist Campground in Siloam Springs, Arkansas. Several hundreds of onlookers and well wishers were present for the organizational meetings.

Three main groups comprised the Fellowship at its organization—a fairly large group of pastors and congregations from the Bible Missionary Church, the entire denomination of the Church of the Bible Covenant, and some independent pastors or churches and parachurch organizations. These groups all had several things in common. One, they were all Wesleyan-Arminian in doctrine. Two, they were convinced of the importance of working together in the Kingdom. Three, they stood for local autonomy for congregations rather than being controlled by a denominational organization. Four, they all desired to return to what they understood to be essential elements of the New Testament church. For them, the organization of the Fellowship signaled a kind of new Reformation—a returning to the Bible for doctrine and polity.

The first Fellowship Assembly elected a 20-person board called the International Coordinating Council (ICC) and a General Secretary. These men had all been part of the original steering committee and had done much of the preparatory work for the organization of the Fellowship. The ICC elected two men to serve as Executive Officers, to head up the organizational aspects of the Fellowship, and to weld the two larger bodies of ministers and churches together into one organizational unit. Rev. Ken Arnold and Dr. Donald Hicks were chosen to lead the organization through the organizational years. Ken Arnold had been influential among the pastors and churches from the Bible Missionary Church, while Dr. Hicks had served the Church of the Bible Covenant in a leadership capacity for more than 20 years—first as president of Covenant Foundation College, and then as General Presiding Officer. His influence led the Church of the Bible Covenant to cast its lot with the Fellowship.

The group of former Bible Missionary pastors and congregations, which were led by Ken Arnold, had left their former affiliation some months prior to the Assembly. They expressed that they intended to be free of autocratic denominational control. They came to the Assembly with the intention of forming an organization which would meet their needs and desires

During the organizational Assembly at Siloam Springs, Dr. Hicks called for a special convention of the Church of the Bible Covenant to discuss and/or vote upon becoming members of the Fellowship. The vote to become part of the International Fellowship of Bible Churches, Inc. was unanimous among the delegates present for the Assembly.

Ken Arnold and Don Hicks were both named CEO, a position they both held until 1991, driving together across the nation and visiting mission works in various places around the world. In early 1991, Ken Arnold resigned his position as CEO. The ICC asked Dr. Hicks to continue in the position of CEO. Dr. Hicks continued to serve as CEO until the 1998 Assembly. In preparation for the Assembly, Dr. Hicks asked the ICC to name William Sillings to the position of CEO in his place. The ICC honored Dr. Hicks' request, electing Dr. Sillings to serve as the Fellowship's next CEO. At the 2002 Assembly, the delegates voted to move from a corporate model of operation to a more ecclesial model by eliminating the positions of General Secretary and CEO and creating the position of General Superintendent. This move is based upon the New Testament concept of an "overseer" or superintendent of the general church, but does not imply organizational authority over the local pastor or the congregation.

Missions

The Fellowship has been a missionary organization from its inception, partly by necessity, and partly because of theology. The theology of the Fellowship is based upon the premise that the Great Commission has not yet been completed, and that the organization itself has a responsibility to help complete the process.

In addition, when the Fellowship was formed, the Church of the Bible Covenant brought with it some mission works operated by the former denomination. There was a clinic, several churches and Bible School in Lesotho, Africa. There was a Bible College and several churches in the Philippines, mainly on Luzon. Robert and Rhonda Gilbert had served the CBC in Guatemala and Mexico, where there were a number of churches, a mission home and some training work being carried on. After serving nearly 20 years on the field, Robert and Rhonda returned to the States to assume responsibilities with Precept Ministries in Chattanooga, TN. Within a year after the Gilberts' return home, Paul Trotzke left his 20 year home in Alaska to serve as our missionary in Guatemala. As well, within a short time after the inception of the Fellowship, churches from Barbados and Guyana announced their desire to join the Fellowship. These churches had been under the auspices of the Bible Missionary Church, but they had separated from the denomination prior to joining the Fellowship.

Currently, Robert Gilbert serves the Fellowship as Director of Missions. The Fellowship operates mission works in the Philippines, Guatemala and Mexico, also assisting churches and pastors in Barbados, Guyana, Haiti and India. As well, the Fellowship is partnering with West Africa Theological Seminary to help train national pastors. WATS is one of Africa's most prestigious seminaries, and the largest Wesleyan-Arminian seminary on the continent.

For Further Reading:

McGrath, Alister. *"I Believe": Exploring the Apostles' Creed.* Downers Grove, IL: InterVarsity, 1997.

Wesley, John. "A Caution against Bigotry," Sermon #38; "Catholic Spirit," Sermon #39.

PART THREE

Fellowship Polity

There can be no dispute that Christ is the head of the universal Church. However, within the headship of Christ, there are variables of church governance. How is the local church to be governed? It is a fundamental belief of the Fellowship that Christ has invested authority in the entire body. To reflect that headship, each local church is an autonomous unit.

Apparently this was the pattern of the early Church. J. A. Seiss, a Lutheran, said the Church was originally congregational [*The Apocalypse,* p. 26]. J. L. Mosheim, a Lutheran historian, wrote, "All the churches, in those primitive times, were independent bodies, or none of them subject to the jurisdiction of any other." John Wesley said, "Originally every Christian congregation was a church independent of all others." Richard Watson wrote, "Through the greater part of the second century the Christian churches were independent of each other" [quoted by Wiley, 3:122-123]. Edward Gibbon wrote that each church was a "little republic" within itself.

Yet the autonomy of the local congregation must be balanced by the concept of inter-dependence among the churches. The apostles did hold a council which set policy for all congregations (Acts 15). Later, the early Church held worldwide or ecumenical councils which clarified Church doctrine.

The body of Christ is a unit. Though it is made up of many parts, they form one body. God did not intend for believers to live in isolation, but to be nurtured in a community of faith. Likewise, God did not intend for congregations to exist in isolation, but to worship in connection with other assemblies of believers and minister to the society in which they exist.

If a triangle could be used to illustrate three models of church government, the top down triangle represents a dictatorship with an episcopal form of government (figure 1). A democracy would be represented by an inverted triangle (figure 2). The congregation elects the board and the board hires the pastor. We recommend a model which puts the triangle on its side (figure 3). The pastor is the equipper at the point of the triangle. He trains lay leaders, who in turn multiply themselves into an army, as the triangle spreads out. This follows the model outlined in Ephesians 4:11-16, which indicates that the work of the leadership of the church is to equip the saints for the work of the ministry.

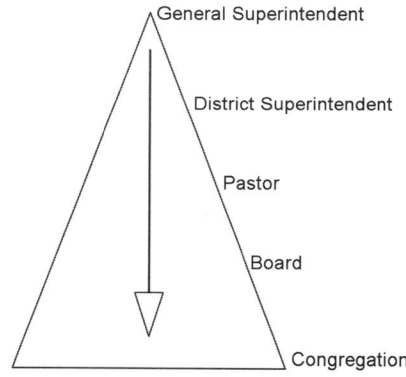

Figure 1 -- Heirarchy Model

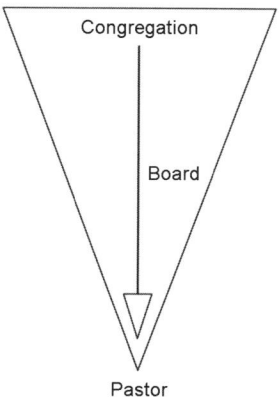

Figure 2 -- Democracy Model

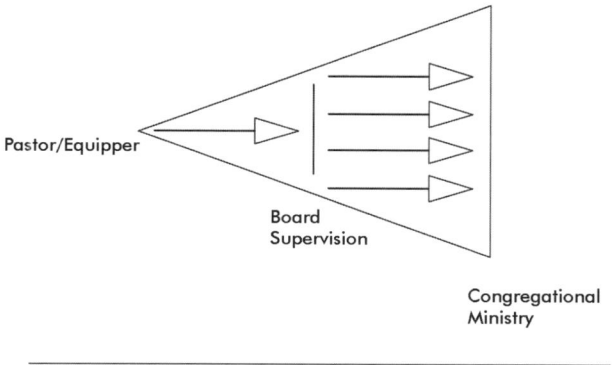

Figure 3 -- Dynamic Ministry Model

Offices of the Church

The Fellowship of Bible Churches recognizes the office of pastor as the highest office in the church. As an organization, the Fellowship exists for the benefit of the local congregation and pastor. There is no hierarchy which must be served by the congregations, yet there is connection and interdependence between the churches themselves, and between the churches and the Fellowship. The International Assembly is a conference of local churches, ministers and parachurch organizations gathered for mutual encouragement and cooperative effort.

The common distinction between clergy and laity, where the clergyman is the minister and the laity are the receivers of ministry, is not a biblical distinction. 1 Peter 2:9 describes the entire Church as a priesthood and as a people belonging to God. It was upon the truth of this passage that Martin Luther developed the theology of the priesthood of all believers. The word "people" is *laos*, from which we get the term "laity." In 1 Peter 5:3 the entire Church is called God's "heritage," or "those entrusted to you." The Greek word used here, *kleros*, is the basis for our word "clergy." In this passage, all God's people are "the clergy."

Furthermore, until recently, in spite of the Reformation's emphasis on the priesthood of all believers, churches have generally believed that professional clergy were hired or called to minister to the "laity." However, all the "clergy," that is, all Christians are to be ministers or servants. The usual word used for ministry is *diakonos*, which is normally translated "deacon." So there is a sense in which all Christians are deacons. Yet the word also has a specialized usage when referring to the office of deacon. God does call leaders to specialized ministry tasks, and the Church does recognize God's call and set apart Christian leaders for specialized ministry. Therefore, the doctrine of the priesthood of all believers does not negate the validity of an ordained ministry.

1. The Office of Pastor-teacher

Pastor-teacher is the term used in Ephesians 4:11 to describe persons who have spiritual oversight of a local congregation. There are three basic headings under which the office of pastor-teacher is described—pastor, bishop and elder. The term "elder" refers to spiritual maturity, the term "bishop" refers to the task of leading, and the term "pastor" refers to the task of feeding.

All three of these headings are found in 1 Peter 5:1-2. "Pastor" is the Latin equivalent to the Greek word for shepherd. "Elders" are to do the work of a pastor-shepherd and to serve as "overseers." The command to watch over the Church is *episkopeo*, the verb form for *episkopos* which is usually translated in the KJV as "bishop." These headings are also located in Acts 20:17. Paul sent for the <u>elders</u>. He charged them in v 28 to guard the flock as overseers or <u>bishops</u> and to be shepherds or <u>pastors</u>.

Two Scriptural passages delineate the required qualifications for this office, 1 Timothy 3:1-7 and Titus 1:6-9. When calling a pastor, the church should seek someone who meets these qualifications, for this person will be their spiritual leader. The pastor is called by God and by the local congregation. By calling the pastor, a congregation is asking explicitly for leadership, and implicitly consenting to follow that leadership.

2. The Office of Deacon

The office of deacon is somewhat ambiguous. The word *diakonos* often is used in the general sense of ministry, but sometimes it refers to a special support ministry for the pastor.

Deacons were first selected in Acts 6, as a supporting role to the Apostles in their ministry as pastor-teacher to the new church. The reason the Apostles called for the selection of "deacons" was so that they could give themselves to prayer and the ministry of the Word. While the word "deacon" is not used in this account, their first assignment was to serve tables (v. 2), and this Greek verb is *diakonein*. This is the verb form for our word "deacon."

By the time Paul addresses the church in Philippi, he addresses two offices of people—bishops and deacons (Phil 1:1). In addition, 1 Timothy 3 is devoted to the qualifications first for bishops, and then for deacons. This demonstrates that by this time, the church had established the office of deacon as an integral part of the ministry of the church. At this time, deacons were fulfilling support roles in the church to the pastor, so that the pastor could continue to give himself to the ministry of the Word and to prayer.

While we do not believe that the Bible requires the ordination of deacons, there is a precedent for this supporting role in the New Testament. When a church decides to set aside persons to the office of deacon, they should seek those who fulfill the requirements delineated in Acts 6:3 and in 1Tim 3:8-13.

3. Other Offices

Ministry is not limited to these two offices. In the New Testament, evangelists, missionaries, and teachers are also commissioned to specialized ministries within the church. These ministers should also be accountable to a local congregation, even though their ministry may extend beyond that local assembly. Ministers have an obligation to watch over each other. They need Christian conference with others in ministry.

In 1752, a group of early Methodist ministers signed a covenant which could serve as a model for accountability among Fellowship ministers.

> That we will not listen or willingly inquire after ill concerning one another; that, if we do hear any ill of each other, we will not be forward to believe it; that as soon as possible we will communicate what we hear by speaking or writing to the person concerned; that until we have done this, we will not write or speak a syllable of it to any other person; that neither will we mention it, after we have done this, to any other person; that we will not make any exception to any of these rules unless we think ourselves absolutely obligated in conference.

The Call of God and the Recognition of the Church

Not only is there the general call of the gospel, which comes to all, there is a vocational call to special ministry that comes to those whom God chooses. Such verses as Romans 1:1 should not be interpreted as the call unto salvation; the call here is the vocational call to ministry.

This inward persuasion that God is setting apart for special ministry should be confirmed by the outward sanction of the church. God both called Samuel, and confirmed that call through Eli and the whole nation of Israel (1 Samuel 3). In this sense, a ministerial license is not permission to preach; rather, it is recognition by the church that God has given a person particular gifts for ministry, and that the minister's life is consistent with the doctrine he preaches. In the New Testament, letters of commendation were sent for Apollos (Acts 18:27), Timothy (1 Cor 16:10-11), Titus (2 Cor 8:18), and Paul (2 Cor 3:1). From these Apostolic examples, we may deduce that God's call to specialized ministry must be both confirmed by giftedness for ministry, and also recognized and approved by the church.

The Ordination Process

Since the Scripture teaches that hands of ordination should not be placed prematurely upon a candidate (1 Tim 5:22), it is fitting that there be a process in which the church discerns God's will for the individual. We require that an applicant for ordination meet for an interview with a credential committee after a minimum of two years of ministry experience.

The purpose of ordination is not to confer merit, and not simply to elevate a person, nor to honor him. It is the recognition of the church that God has called an individual, and that his life and doctrine is consistent with that call. Thus, ordination does not represent a transfer of power, but a recognition of God's call and of one's spiritual, mental, moral and emotional fitness for ministry. Oden states that the laying on of hands combines the themes of acknowledgment of divine calling, appointment, entrustment, consecration, public blessing and intercession for divine assistance and discernment, commissioning, and sending forth to office [*Classic Pastoral Care*, Vol. 1 *Becoming a Minister*, Baker, 1987, p. 116].

We believe a minister should be ordained by a group of his peers. In the Fellowship, this group is called the Fellowship of Elders.

While every rule has its exception, the walk to ordination within the International Fellowship of Bible Churches, Inc. generally follows the pathway shown below.

Step One: The minister senses the call of God on his life.

Step Two: Others in the church recognize the same call, and encourage the minister to continue to develop.

Step Three: The called one begins to prepare himself for the work of the ministry, including exercising his ministry gifts within the scope of the church's ministry.

Step Four: The minister applies to the Fellowship for Minister's License and/or ordination. The Fellowship currently recognizes two levels of licensing. The Minister's License is a temporary license granted to the person preparing toward ordination. The licensed minister is interviewed, encouraged and held accountable for progress toward completion of preparation for ordination. Ordination is granted as a more-or-less permanent (not unconditional) recognition of one's readiness and fitness for ministry.

Step Five: The minister works through the ordination workbook and tapes.

Step Six: The minster completes the written essays over the material.

Step Seven: The minister is given a final interview by a Credentials Examination Committee and recommendation is made to the Fellowship of Elders with regard to granting ordination.

Step Eight: The minister is approved by the Fellowship of Elders at the Assembly immediately following the completion of the processes outlined above.

Step Nine: The candidate is formally ordained at an ordination service, either at the Assembly or in his local church, by a presbytery of ordaining elders. He is then presented with a gold seal certificate of his ordination.

In the credentials examination interviews, the candidate for minister's license and/or ordination will be asked such questions as the following. Of course, not all these questions will be asked of any one candidate, but they represent the kinds of questions which may be asked.

The purpose of the interview is to discern the ordination candidate's readiness for ministry, as well as his/her compatibility with the doctrines and practices of the International Fellowship of Bible Churches, Inc. It is not intended to be a personal grilling session, but a time of gracious rapport and support between and toward new ministers.

Section 1 Personal, Spiritual

1. Please state your testimony of your personal relationship with Christ.

2. Tell us about your call into the ministry. Do you believe God has called you into the ministry?

3. What do you believe to be the nature of your call? That is, what do you believe God wants you to do as a result of his call on your life?

Section 2 Marital, Family

1. What is your marital status?

2. What is your spouse's reaction to your being in the ministry? How does your spouse support your decision to enter into the ministry?

3. Do your children support your ministry? Do they believe in your readiness for the ministry?

4. How will being in the ministry affect your family management or quality of family life?

5. Is there anything in your family life which you believe will be a detriment to your ministry?

Section 3 Financial

1. Have you fulfilled your personal financial obligations and kept your business contracts?

2. What do you believe about indebtedness?

3. How does your level of indebtedness affect your ministry?

4. What do you believe the Bible teaches about stewardship? (short statement)

5. Do you set an example by tithing your income?

Section 4 Doctrinal

1. What is your view of authority of Scripture?

2. What is your conviction about the major tenets of the Christian faith as reflected in the historic Creeds?

    a. Explain your understanding of the relationships between the persons of the Godhead.

    b. What is your conviction about the deity of Christ?

    c. What do you believe about the virgin birth of Jesus Christ?

    d. What do you believe about the death of Christ as an atonement for our sins?

    e. What do you believe about the bodily resurrection of Christ?

    f. What do you believe about the second coming of Christ?

    g. What do you believe about justification by faith?

    h. What is your understanding of the indwelling of the Holy Spirit?

    i. What do you believe about the nature and work of sanctification?

    j. What do you believe about holiness of heart and life?

    k. What do you understand to be the nature of the church and its relationship to Christ?

    l. What do you believe about the mission of the church? What is your commitment to the Great Commission? What social issues do you believe your congregation needs to address in order to minister to its community?

Section 5 Pastoral

1. Tell us about your ministry experience.

2. Give an example of an encounter with a difficulty or problem in the church, and explain what you did to minister to that situation.

3. If you were to encounter the same kind of situation again, would you do anything differently? If so, what would you do?

Section 6 Organizational

1. What local church currently holds your membership?

2. What has led you to seek affiliation and/or licensing with the Fellowship of Bible Churches?

3. What do you see as your contribution to the Fellowship?

4. What do you see as the Fellowship's contribution to your life and ministry?

5. Will you support the Fellowship financially?

6. Do you understand and are you committed to our mission statement?

7. Are you in harmony with the Fellowship's Handbook of Faith and Practice?

Section 7 Miscellaneous

1. What is your attitude toward accountability? To whom are you currently accountable and how is that accountability carried out?

2. Who is influencing you?
    a. What books have you read recently?
    b. What tapes have you listened to recently?
    c. What videos have you watched within the past few months?

    d.   What conferences have you attended within the last year?

3. Is there anything in your life which, if known, would prevent us from granting your request for license or ordination?

4. Is there anything you want to ask of us?

For Further Reading:

Oden, Thomas C. *Pastoral Theology.* San Francisco: Harper and Row, 1983. Chapters 2-3, "The Call to Ministry" and "The Meaning of Ordination."

Oden, Thomas C. *Classic Pastoral Care.* Volume One, *Becoming a Minister.* Grand Rapids: Baker, 1987. Chapter 1, "The Pastoral Calling."

General Operations

The Fellowship of Bible Churches is a support organization for pastors and churches. While we recognize the autonomy of each congregation, the international organization of the Fellowship enables many local congregations to work together for the common good and for increased effectiveness in completing the Great Commission. Thus, the Fellowship is purposely organized to complement the work of the local church rather than to compete with it. What follows is an overview of our structure as an international organization.

International Assembly

The International Assembly (and Family Camp) meets every two years on the even numbered year for the purposes of caring for Fellowship business, electing officers, promoting Fellowship purposes and goals, spiritual refreshment and renewing of fellowship among friends. Business is generally cared for quickly, with the majority of the time spent together devoted to camp services, spiritual renewal and the like.

The International Assembly is the final authority in matters pertaining to the Fellowship as an organization. At each Assembly, delegates elect a General Superintendent of the Fellowship, a 20 member board called the International Coordinating Council, and the Nominating Committee for the next Assembly's work. They also approve any changes which need to be made in the handbook and approve financial and general reports.

General Superintendent

The General Superintendent is elected by the Assembly to lead the Fellowship and to oversee the work and activities of the Fellowship. He works in connection with the ICC and the Executive Committee. He is the chairman of the ICC, the Executive Committee and the International Assembly.

Missions Director

The Fellowship of Bible Churches operates or supports mission work in Central America, Mexico, Barbados, Guyana, Haiti, the Philippines and Nigeria. The Missions Director has direct oversight of Fellowship missions, serving under the direction of the General Superintendent and the ICC.

Fellowship Pastoral Consultant

When Dr. Donald Hicks resigned as CEO of the Fellowship in 1998, the ICC saw in his ministry a valuable resource for pastors and churches. The ICC unanimously voted to ask Dr. Hicks to continue to travel across the country for the Fellowship, encouraging pastors and meeting with churches to promote the interests of the Fellowship.

International Coordinating Council

The International Coordinating Council (ICC), is a 20 member board elected by the International Asssembly. The ICC cares for business matters between Assemblies, and their work is amenable to the Assembly itself.

The ICC is comprised of 10 elders and 10 laymen, plus the General Superintendent. The Superintendent of Missions and the Fellowship Pastoral Consultant are also *ex officio* members of the ICC.

Executive Committee

The Executive Committee is comprised of a small number of members of the ICC, charged with the responsibility to work with the General Superintendent between ICC meetings. Their work is largely administrative, while the ICC sets policy and direction. Members of the Executive Committee are selected by the General Superintendent and approved by the ICC.

Fellowship of Elders

The Fellowship of Elders is comprised of all ordained elders within the Fellowship of Bible Churches. The Fellowship of Elders meets at each International Assembly and is the body responsible for approving candidates for Minister's License and/or Ordination.

Funding

The Fellowship of Bible Churches raises its funding on a voluntary basis. The Fellowship currently uses two major streams of funding for its projects. One is missions funding, the other is general funding.

Missions funding is accomplished in various ways. Two times a year, at Easter and Thanksgiving, the missions work of the Fellowship asks churches and individuals for a significant offering for missions work. These two offerings comprise the major lifelines for Fellowship Missions funding. In addition, special approved projects are advertised at other times of the year for those who wish to take on all or part of a project for a particular field need.

Funding for the general operation of the Fellowship is currently raised in two ways. One, churches are solicited for a percentage of their income from their tithes and offerings. While these offerings are just that – offerings and not budgets—we all realize that it takes a significant amount of funding to manage the Fellowship at the organizational level, even though we have a minimal internal operational budget.

The second method of funding is the Fellowship Ministers' Share. The Fellowship asks ministers licensed or ordained by the Fellowship to show their good faith interest in the work of the Fellowship by supporting the Fellowship on a monthly basis. This may be part of their tithe, a special offering through the local church, or just a special offering from the minister himself. We believe the Fellowship as an organization provides a meaningful ministry to us as ministers, and that the Fellowship is worthy of our financial support on a consistent basis.

Ministerial Discipline

While we pray that ministerial discipline will never be necessary among our beloved ministers, such discipline has sometimes been necessary in the past in order to correct character or moral flaws, and/or to restore ministers to full faith, their families to full relationship, and their ministries to full effectiveness. Therefore, we set forth the following guidelines for ministerial discipline within the International Fellowship of Bible Churches, Inc.

1. Ministerial discipline within the International Fellowship of Bible Churches, Inc. will be administered through a Disciplinary Committee, comprised of no fewer than five elders from the ICC, and appointed by the ICC.

2. Ministerial discipline shall be a matter of utmost confidentiality. Betrayal of confidentiality by a member of the disciplinary committee, in and of itself, may be considered sufficient grounds for disciplinary action toward the committee member.

3. Before any minister shall be required to undergo disciplinary action, actual proof of wrongdoing must be ascertained without violation of any principles laid out in Chapter Seven of the ***Handbook of Faith and Practice.***

4. If a minister seeks to transfer into the Fellowship during a disciplinary action by another credentialing agency, the general course of action will be to cooperate with the minister's disciplining agency. With perhaps an extremely rare exception, any transfer of licensing will be postponed until the period of discipline is completed, in order not to undermine the authority of the ordaining board who is more aware of the subtleties of the case.

5. Should a minister seek a transfer out of the Fellowship during a disciplinary action, a letter of transfer may be given, but only if accompanied by an adequate explanation of the disciplinary action being taken in the minister's behalf.

6. Ministerial discipline may be administered in cases where the minister has abandoned the Scriptural qualifications of elders as they are listed in 2 Timothy and Titus, or where the minister's life violates the principles of moral and spiritual rectitude in some other significant manner.

7. Ministerial discipline will be based upon the following philosophy:

    a. There is neither claim to, nor expectation of personal perfection among Fellowship ministers. The Fellowship believes in, teaches and practices biblical holiness. However, within the spectrum of theology and practice, there is a wide diversity of application of belief. And as a theological principle, the Fellowship typically makes a little more allowance for imperfection, though not for sin, than many of its Wesleyan-Arminian denominational sisters. Nevertheless, since ministers are in such positions of influence and power, the Fellowship cannot show lack of due diligence when the minister's life is clearly out of balance with Scriptural precedent. That being stated, however, even in cases where discipline is necessary, every disciplinary action should be taken in the spirit of humility and restoration (Gal 6:1-2).

    b. Since the International Fellowship of Bible Churches, Inc. is a Fellowship and not a denomination, it assumes a perspective on ministerial discipline which is unique from that of many denominational organizations. With only biblical principle to be concerned about, the Fellowship enjoys the freedom to do what is biblically necessary or advisable.

c. The Fellowship has purposely chosen to aim for biblical balance in all matters, which, in the case of ministerial discipline, means judging each case on its own merit. Generally speaking, a minister may be called into question for disciplinary measures whenever he is known to transgress the biblical principles laid out in 2 Timothy and Titus, where Paul deals with the qualifications for elders within the church. Proof of abandonment or significant violation of these principles shall be considered sufficient grounds for disciplinary action.

d. Ministerial discipline shall always be based on biblically sound principle and shall seek the protection and restoration of the minister, his family and his ministry. No set system guarantees "if you follow these rules you can be fully restored to ministry." Of course, this does not make so neat a package to deal with, as there may be in cases where rules have proliferated. But this kind of policy throws the Fellowship back on the authority of Scripture and the leadership of the Holy Spirit to make courageous Scriptural applications.

e. It is a principle of operation within the Fellowship that any ministerial discipline will be aimed at faithfulness to Scriptural principle, while simultaneously working diligently for the redemption and restoration of the minister's life, family, and ministry.

f. Consequently, no disciplinary action is to be taken as punishment, but is always to be regarded as a means to complete restoration of the person, family, and/or ministry of the minister—or all three, as the case may demand.

g. With that stated, it is also necessary to state that each case is unique. As a general rule, however, in any disciplinary action, the disciplinary committee will be looking for the following characteristics in the minister:

   1). Full admission/confession of any wrong doing, or substantiated claims that the charges are false.

2). An attitude of humility without self justification.

3). A sense that the minister, if guilty, is truly repentant, not merely embarrassed and sorry he was found out.

4). A sense that his wife and family are surviving the misconduct intact and are in agreement to support the minister throughout the process of restoration.

5). Willingness to undergo the required steps to full restoration, including, if necessary, counseling and accountability structures.

6). An assurance, mainly from the minister's attitude, that the problem will not be repeated.

7). Submission to the authority of the disciplinary committee, without impatience or impertinence.

8). Willingness to submit to professional counsel, where deemed necessary by the committee.

9). Cooperation with a local church board in the restoration process, where applicable.

Once again, it is necessary to state that this part of this course is concerned only with cases where disciplinary action is called for or deemed necessary and appropriate. It is also important to understand that this procedure is a general procedure. While the spirit of these guidelines may not be violated, specific items may be altered if it is determined that such alteration will effect a better outcome.

CONCLUSION

You have just finished working through an introductory treatment of the basic doctrines and polity of the International Fellowship of Bible Churches, Inc. Congratulations!

Before you lay this book aside, may we, the authors, encourage you to continue your journey into the Scriptures and theological study? Some of the themes presented in this book are fathomless truths which this short treatment could not begin to treat sufficiently. The study of the Scriptures and the doctrines that arise from it are life-long pursuits.

There is a story about Alexander Maclaren, great Scottish expositor of the 19th century, which bears repeating here. Maclaren was known to have devoted sixty hours to the preparation of a single message. He studied early in the morning to lunch. Then back in the study after noon for an hour or two. The afternoon was given to other duties of the church. After dinner, he sat in his rocking chair with a copy of the Scriptures in the original languages, pouring over God's holy Word so as to know God better. He was invited, but refused to deliver the Yale Lectures on preaching, and he also refused most other guest speaking engagements, preferring to remain in Manchester and to preach to his people. He preached in Manchester for forty-five years, giving rise to the name "Maclaren of Manchester."

Maclaren was a preacher of unusual knowledge and insight. But no wonder. He literally saturated himself with the Word of God until his sermons came from the overflow of his mind and heart. He spent hours in meditation on both the Old and New Testaments, seeking to know the mind and heart of

God ever better. Before he ever preached a text, he sought first to apply it to himself, and only then to his people.

While we may shrink back in awe of such a unique character, thinking we could never arise to such heights as Maclaren, we need not wander through life without honing our knowledge, skills and spiritual depth to our potential. And who knows, some of our readers may indeed rise to the heights of a Maclaren, or a Wesley, or an Asbury. There is nothing to prevent our trying to be at our best, both spiritually and mentally, as well as theologically and practically.

If anything prevents us from reaching our greatest potential for God, it will likely be the frenetic pace and the petty duties of our day. It will be because we have placed too high a priority on the accouterments of church life and not enough on the biblical, theological and spiritual. Therefore, the two of us would like to join the Apostle Paul in issuing you this challenge—"Make every effort to show yourself approved unto God, a workman that needs not to be ashamed, rightly dividing the Word of truth" (2 Tim 2:15).

> Yours in Christ,
>
> William Sillings and Vic Reasoner